The Lord's Supper
is a celebration of grace

The Lord's Supper
is a celebration of grace

What the Bible teaches about communion

Gordon J. Keddie

EVANGELICAL PRESS
Faverdale North Industrial Estate, Darlington, DL3 0PH, England

Evangelical Press USA
P. O. Box 84, Auburn, MA 01501, USA

e-mail: sales@evangelical-press.org

web: www.evangelical-press.org

First published 2000

British Library Cataloguing in Publication Data available

ISBN 0 85234 425 2

Printed and bound in Great Britain by Creative Print & Design Wales, Ebbw Vale

Contents

Preface

Alongside the preaching of the Word of God, the Lord's Supper ought to be central in the life of the church and of each and every professing Christian. Here is where the believer meets with the Saviour in a vivid way, by means of a symbolic feast in which the food and drink represent the sacrificial death of Jesus Christ on the cross of Calvary.

Understanding the meaning of the Lord's Supper is essential to enjoying its blessings. Too often, the Lord's Supper is treated as a mere given, an assumption of church life — ostensibly a highlight but largely taken for granted. The result in practice is that it is left to be whatever people make of it, a highly individual experience undirected by any concerted effort by the church to expound what that experience ought to be in the life of the communicant.

This little book attempts to fill the need for such an exposition. These chapters began as part of a series of sermons on 1 Corinthians preached in Grace Reformed

Presbyterian Church, State College, PA. They are here presented in published form in the hope that they will be helpful in giving greater meaning to the experience of the Lord's Supper for the people of God. The same grace is conveyed in the Supper as in any other of the means of grace. This is true, whether in the Word, the sacraments, or prayer. But, in the Supper, the focus is so finely drawn around the cross that the centrality of Christ as the substitute sacrifice for sinners inescapably fills the horizon of our reflection and adoration. Should this, then, not lead us to desire and to anticipate his richest blessing of our souls whenever we commune with him under the symbols of his broken body and his shed blood? May the Lord so bless us, 'till he comes' (1 Cor. 11:26).

Gordon J. Keddie
State College, PA
July 2000

For I received from the Lord that which I also delivered to you: that the Lord Jesus on the same night in which he was betrayed took bread; and when he had given thanks, he broke it and said, 'Take, eat; this is my body which is broken for you; do this in remembrance of me.' In the same manner he also took the cup after supper, saying, 'This cup is the new covenant in my blood. This do, as often as you drink it, in remembrance of me.' For as often as you eat this bread and drink this cup, you proclaim the Lord's death till he comes.

Therefore whoever eats this bread or drinks this cup of the Lord in an unworthy manner will be guilty of the body and blood of the Lord. But let a man examine himself, and so let him eat of the bread and drink of the cup. For he who eats and drinks in an unworthy manner eats and drinks judgement to himself, not discerning the Lord's body. For this reason many are weak and sick among you, and many sleep. For if we would judge ourselves, we would not be judged. But when we are judged, we are chastened by the Lord, that we may not be condemned with the world.

Therefore, my brethren, when you come together to eat, wait for one another. But if anyone is hungry, let him eat at home, lest you come together for judgement. And the rest I will set in order when I come

(1 Cor. 11:23-34).

1.
Consecration

'For I received from the Lord that which I also delivered to you: that the Lord Jesus on the same night in which he was betrayed took bread; and when he had given thanks, he broke it and said, "Take, eat; this is my body which is broken for you; do this in remembrance of me"' (1 Cor. 11:23-24).

In one of his famous 'Princeton sermons', Charles Hodge observed that we 'cannot commemorate Christ as our Saviour without thereby acknowledging ourselves to be his, the purchase of his blood and devoted to his service'.[1] The Lord's Supper is, in its very nature, an ordinance that claims our *hearts* now and commands our *consecration* henceforth. The apostle Paul captures something of that flavour of the permanent and abiding character of a genuine Christian commitment when he encourages the church with the exhortation: 'For as often as you eat this bread and drink this cup, you proclaim the Lord's death till he comes' (1 Cor. 11:26).

The first thing to grasp is that the Lord's Supper is *for professing Christians to profess afresh their faith in Christ.* Coming to the Lord's Table is for believers in Christ, and believers only. 'Dead men must not sit down at the Table of the living God,' said Thomas Doolittle.[2] The right receiving of the elements, as we shall see in greater detail later, necessarily involves a personal heart-commitment to Jesus Christ, an affirmation of the efficacy of the cross and a desire to confess him before heaven and earth as 'my Lord and my God' (John 20:28). Faithful participation is *evangelical*, in that it is prompted by a heart transformed by the *evangel* (i.e., the gospel); and it is *evangelistic*, in that it proclaims to the watching world — and, make no mistake, the world is watching what the church is doing — that this same Saviour is the one whom all people everywhere need to know about, believe in and come to follow.

To argue, as some have done, that the presence of Judas Iscariot at the institution of the Supper proves that unbelievers may be admitted to the Table misses the mark. Judas was, up to that point, a professing disciple of Jesus, was regarded as such by his brethren and was taken at face value by our Lord himself. That he was a hypocrite only underscores the fact that a credible profession of faith can sometimes mask an unbelieving heart. For long enough, Judas no doubt thought of himself as a sincere follower of Jesus, but that Passover night he knew he was only playing the part of a disciple. As the betrayer of Jesus, he affords us the 'worst case' example of what it can mean when 'he who eats and drinks in an unworthy manner eats and drinks judgement to himself'.

Secondly, the Lord's Supper is an observance by which God means *to strengthen and confirm believers in their devotion to the Lord*. The Westminster *Shorter Catechism* expresses this well:

Question: What are the outward means whereby Christ communicate[s] to us the benefits of redemption?

Answer: The outward and ordinary means whereby Christ communicate[s] to us the benefits of redemption, are his ordinances, especially the word, sacraments, and prayer; all which are made effectual to the elect for salvation

(Question 88).

The Lord's Supper is one of the 'sacraments' of which the catechism speaks, the other being baptism. The word 'sacrament' is not a biblical term, but derives from the Latin *sacramentum*, which variously referred to something holy and mysterious — i.e., having a deeper underlying spiritual reality to it. The oath taken by a Roman soldier was called a *sacramentum*, thus indicating a deeper level of commitment than that of, say, a mere employee. The essential point in relation to the Supper is that the powerful grace of God accompanies this ordinance — this 'means of grace' — to the end that the believer's present and future consecration to the Lord may be secured.

Thirdly, the Lord's Supper is *an inescapably corporate experience*. No one can administer it to himself. It belongs to the people of God, as a people gathered to worship and serve the Lord according to his revealed will. The fact that it takes the form of a meal emphasizes the aspect of fellowship around the Table, as people of 'like precious faith' receive spiritual nourishment from the Saviour who is 'the bread of life' (John 6:35).

The power of the Lord's Supper

The Christian church, then, has always understood the sacraments, along with the preaching of the Word of God and prayer in the life of the believer, to be *means of grace*. That is to say that God, by these means, projects his enabling and transforming power into the lives of the participants. As one of these means, the Lord's Supper is designed to accomplish certain practical goals consonant with the gracious purposes of God for his people.

One thing it is *not* designed to do, however, is to make people Christians. It is not designed to *convert* people to Christ. It is not a 'converting ordinance', to be dispensed to the unbelieving in the hope of bringing them to Christ. The witness of the Christian in communing is an evangelistic witness, but the Supper itself is not an evangelistic tool. In contrast to the preaching of the Word, which is a converting ordinance to be dispensed to both unbelievers and believers, the Lord's Supper is clearly directed to those who are *already* believers. It has the role of confirming the faith that is being proclaimed by the communicants. It is therefore to be regarded as a 'confirming ordinance'. The Supper is intended to stir up personal godliness and spiritual growth in already committed Christians.

This spiritual growth results from the work of the Holy Spirit in and through the sacrament, as it is faithfully received. It does not happen automatically. There is no magic in the Lord's Supper. The mere ingestion of the bread and wine conveys no blessing. The Corinthian Christians attended many communion services and partook of a great deal of bread and wine, but, in doing so as they did, they actually denied God's power, with the result that he withheld his power and visited them in righteous judgement (1 Cor. 11:30). God deals with us as responsible individuals and expects us to take him seriously. The mystery of the operations of his power in the Supper is that, in Hodge's words, 'The condition of this power, on our part, is faith. That is, if we have faith, we experience the power of the sacrament; if we have it not, we do not experience it.'[3]

The power of the Holy Spirit is operative in connection with the Lord's Supper as a visible gospel word that derives all its content and meaning from the written Word of God. The context of the institution of the Lord's Supper was Jesus' instruction of his disciples in the so-called Supper Discourse (John 14-16), teaching in which he spoke of the coming of the Holy Spirit who would lead them into all truth (John 16:13). This is why the preaching of the Word should always precede the administration of the sacrament. Without the Scriptures, the sacraments would be reduced to bare symbols and arbitrary ritual, shorn of their true significance and hostage to the subjective inventiveness of their uncomprehending practitioners — something that is already widespread in churches that have lost their scriptural moorings. By the power of the Word and the Holy Spirit, the Lord in the Supper confirms to faithfully participating believers the forgiveness of their sin and their redemption through his sacrificial death. And what are the contours of that experience? They come to enjoy, to one degree or another, a deepening sense of union with Christ. This is marked by a growing fellowship with other

Christians, and a strengthening of faith and confidence as redeemed people who know what it is to have eternal life in Jesus.[4]

Our future obedience

Because the Lord's Supper focuses on the *death* of Jesus and brings us, as it were, to the foot of the cross, it also leads us to the empty tomb and the claims of the *risen* Saviour. Jesus is no longer either on the cross or in the tomb. He suffered, died and rose again from the dead to become the exalted Mediator, the Redeemer of God's elect, the Saviour of the lost and the Head over all things to the church. What flows from the cross is *new life* in a risen Saviour. To miss that point in the Lord's Supper is to miss what it is saying to us about all our tomorrows.

Over a century ago, Henry Belfrage of Falkirk (Scotland) exhorted his people, 'In eating this bread, and drinking this cup, you have been acknowledging the obligations which His death lays upon you to serve Him. You have been giving a solemn pledge, in the face of heaven and earth, that you will labour to promote the great moral purposes of His sufferings. You have declared that you will crucify the flesh, with its affections and lusts; that you will never listen to the temptations which may solicit you to abandon the Saviour; that on your heads, the guilt of apostasy shall never be charged; and that to deny yourselves, to take up your cross and follow Him, is the purpose of your hearts, and the business of your lives.'[5]

Yet for millions in this world, the Lord's Supper, or what passes for it in some churches, is often the only religious observance left in their lives, and a sadly perfunctory performance at that. Between 'communion Sundays' there is often no observable devotion, or even regular church attendance. The rest of life is relentlessly religionless, or even downright irreligious, and therefore effectively devoid of any spiritual content. Even their observance of communion is routine and lifeless, the creature of ingrained habit rather than the effervescent enthusiasm of a deeply felt love for the Lord.

Each believer is to confess with humility of mind and exalted comprehension that it is 'no longer I who live, but Christ lives in me' (Gal. 2:20). Anything less — a cold, mechanical, unfelt ritual observance — is a tragic, empty substitute for the real thing and indicative of a heart that is not right with God. Erstwhile communicants need to answer some very practical questions. What use will you make of the Lord's Supper in the coming week? Have you felt its claims upon your pattern of life? Has the Lord Jesus Christ not spoken to your heart in the Supper? Do you love Christ? Are you, right now, trusting yourself to him as your Saviour and Lord?

Ponder also the fact that putting into practice the clear moral and spiritual claims of the Supper must tend to stop the mouths of those who despise the gospel. Fresh resolve to follow Christ proves the sincerity of the communicants' faith. The scandal is that millions go to the Lord's Table and contradict its meaning in daily life without seeing any problem. Here is where the subtlety of Satan is clearly seen.

Why is it that in churches with large nominal memberships, the Lord's Supper is one of the very few events that get people into church? Surely it is that Satan may mock Jesus by showing up the scandalous inconsistency of people who live like pagans in between the supposed 'communions' they so assiduously attend.

Consider afresh what Jesus Christ has done. Did he suffer just for us to pamper ourselves with self-satisfied neglect of his claims? Did he die for us to be easy with our sinful ways? Did he rise from the grave so that we should go on living for ourselves with scarcely a thought about sin, righteousness and judgement to come?

Tests of sincerity

In his first letter, the apostle John makes the point that when we are brought under the searchlight of God's righteousness, the honest and realistic response is confession of sin: 'If we say that we have not sinned, we make him a liar, and his word is not in us' (1 John 1:10).

Confession of sin is fine, but it is not the same thing as personal godliness, so John takes pains to assure his readers that the goal of such confession is that they might not sin: 'My little children, these things I write to you, so that you may not sin. And if anyone sins, we have an Advocate with the Father, Jesus Christ the righteous. And he himself is the propitiation for our sins, and not for ours only but also for the whole world. Now by this we know that we know him, if we keep his commandments' (1 John 2:1-3).

Notice the transition between verses 2 and 3. In verse 2, Jesus is the 'propitiation for our sins' — that is, he satisfies the holy anger of God against our sin, by which he becomes favourable (i.e., propitious) towards us. In verse 3, this is held to require that we actually 'keep his commandments' in daily life. In other words, knowing Christ truly as Saviour issues in obeying him seriously as Lord. There is no possibility of the one without the other. They constitute a unitary experience of saving grace and its fruit. In succeeding verses, the apostle describes a number of tests that may be applied to show whether we are truly trusting in the Saviour:

Test 1: We know that we know God *if* we keep his commandments (1 John 2:3-4).
Test 2: We see God's love perfected in us *if* we keep his word (1 John 2:5).
Test 3: We truly abide in him *if* we walk as Christ walked (1 John 2:5-6).

Notice how John takes us from the death of Christ, as the substitutionary sacrifice propitiating the justified anger of God against sinners (v. 2), to evidential fruit in sinners who have truly believed in the Son of God (vv. 3-6). The 'proof of the pudding' is in the eating. The very phraseology employed in verse 3 — 'By this we know that we know him' — challenges us with the vital question: 'Do you really know the Lord?' Do you evidence the 'this' ('Now by *this* ...', v. 3) that shows that you know Jesus in the power of the resurrection?

In the Lord's Supper, then, we are brought to the cross and charged to consecrate ourselves afresh to Christ. What other than personal consecration shall we render to the Lord for all the benefits he has bestowed upon us? (Ps. 116:12). To be sure, we are not worthy of the least of them, and never shall be, left to ourselves (Gen. 32:10). But, in him, we shall be 'more than conquerors through him who loved us' (Rom. 8:37). We 'love him because he first loved us' (1 John 4:19). Because we love him, we will keep his commandments (John 14:15). And we will do so with the glad gratitude of those who know what it is to be lost and then found, dead and then made alive. And this is all through the grace of the one and only Saviour, Jesus Christ, who died that sinners such as we are should not perish, but have everlasting life.

2.
Visible signs

'For as often as you eat this bread and drink this cup, you proclaim the Lord's death till he comes' (1 Cor. 11:26).

If Paul had written his First Epistle to the Corinthians *specifically* to your church, you would by now be smarting under his rebukes. Problem after problem surfaces in this letter. In chapters 11-14, he discusses the *order* of the church — not in the manner of an academic course of lectures, but as the most pointed correction of practical abuses in the church addressed to the consciences of the members. In 11:17-22, he revisits the *disunity* with which he began in the first chapter. Evidently, they had meals together as a church. This was the *agape*, or 'love feast'. These communal meals were supposed to unite people, but they ended up demonstrating the disunity and selfishness of the Corinthian church.

Then, in full flight of dissension and even dissipation (11:21), the members sat down at the Lord's Table! How they imagined that this travesty of sacramental observance could be pleasing to God and a blessing to themselves is beyond all understanding. Since their actual behaviour flew in the face of the meaning of Christ's death, of the claims of the gospel and of practical Christian life, their 'communion' was a virtual trampling on the Saviour whom they professed to have saved them *from* their sins. They were already under the judgements of God (11:30), but so great was their state of denial that they were the last to discern their own desperate spiritual condition.

Now, what is the Lord's Supper supposed to do for the church? It is certainly not to be an empty ritual where people *pretend* to be united *to* Christ and to be one *in* Christ, while their hearts are far from him and from each other. The Supper, as we have already seen, is supposed to be a means of *grace*, not an occasion of self-centredness and drunkenness![1] Let us notice, first, what the Lord's Supper is to be to us — a *means of grace*; and, secondly, how the Lord's Supper fulfils its intended purpose in us — through *visible signs*.

A means of grace

The essential idea of the Lord's Supper is summed up in Paul's commentary on the institution of the sacrament: 'For as often as you eat this bread and drink this cup, you proclaim the Lord's death till he comes' (1 Cor. 11:26). On the face of it, the focus here seems to be very much upon what the communicants are doing, namely, eating and drinking and proclaiming with respect to Christ's death. It would be a mistake, however, to think of this exclusively in terms of human action. Why? Because it is in fact conditioned by the sovereign initiatives of the free grace of

God, by which men and women come to believe in Christ in the first place, and then continue to grow spiritually as he feeds them thereafter with the bread of life. God acts in the Supper, precisely as the Holy Spirit speaking in the Word applies the truth represented in the sacrament to the believer's heart, mind and conscience. God acts in our actions, as these are faithfully expressed in our coming to the Supper. God enacts our blessing, as we receive Christ spiritually under the symbols of his atoning death which we receive physically. His grace is conveyed to the believing soul, as he or she comes obediently, willingly and discerningly to the Table of the Lord.

What is this grace of which the Supper is a 'means'?

When we say that grace is conveyed in the Lord's Supper, we must be clear as to what we mean by 'grace'. When the Bible speaks about grace, it does so in a number of different ways.

Objectively, grace is variously described as: an *attribute* of God's character ('the God of all grace,' 1 Peter 5:10); an *attitude* of God towards particular people ('Do not be afraid, Mary, for you have found favour [grace] with God,' Luke 1:30); or the *unmerited favour* of God in justifying sinners ('For by grace you have been saved through faith, and that not of yourselves…' Eph. 2:8).

Subjectively, grace is that power of God that we experience acting upon our hearts, when God, by his Holy Spirit accompanying the Word, convicts us, converts us, changes us and confirms us through the gospel of Christ. This happens under the *preaching* of the Word: 'So then faith comes by hearing, and hearing by the word of God' (Rom. 10:17). 'Sanctify them by your truth,' Jesus asks the Father. 'Your word is truth' (John 17:17). It also takes place in connection with the *sacraments*, baptism and the Lord's Supper. These visibly illustrate the written Word of God, by using signs to seal God's promises to his people. God conveys his grace to his people as they participate in a believing manner.

What happens in the Lord's Supper?

Several things happen in the interaction between the Lord and his people, as they faithfully partake of the Supper.

1. Believers confess afresh their faith in Jesus Christ

They 'proclaim' the Lord's death and renew their personal covenant with their Saviour (1 Cor. 11:26).

From the perspective of the *individual communicant*, this is nothing less than a personal confession before the Lord, the church and the world, of Christ as Saviour and Lord. To partake of the bread and the cup is to give public testimony to personal faith in, and commitment to, the crucified and risen Jesus. A cold, ritual participation is a travesty. Without devotion to Christ from the heart, and an enthusiastic resolve to be his disciple, there is no reason to expect any blessing from God. Without faith, it is impossible to please God (Heb. 11:6).

As a symbolic feast, the Supper also has a profound *corporate dimension*. It draws believers together in the fellowship of Christ's saving work as they confess the same Lord and the same faith. It is a covenant bond of union horizontally as well as vertically. This was routinely flouted by the Corinthians in their divisions (1 Cor. 11:18), factions (11:19) and shaming of those who had nothing (11:22), and was the trigger for the judgements which God visited upon them (11:30). They should therefore 'wait for one another' (11:33), and so come together in the unity of heart and practice implicit in properly 'discerning the Lord's body' (11:29). Thomas Doolittle asks, 'Does not this ordinance, which shows you the love of Christ for all His people, incite those who attend upon it to imitate the Lord Jesus in loving them? Does the Supper not show you that we should love one another as He has loved us, when we see we are one body, redeemed by one Lord and fed at one Table; that we are washed in the same blood, enjoy the same privileges, and here are assured of the same inheritance and glory?'[2]

2. Believers commune with Jesus Christ

Jesus is 'the bread of God ... who comes down from heaven and gives life to the world ... the bread of life,' and he tells us that 'He who comes to me shall never hunger, and he who believes in me shall never thirst' (John 6:33-35). In the Supper, Christ feeds believers under the symbol of the elements of bread and wine. There is a spiritual communion, a feeding on Christ by the Holy Spirit and through faith in him. On the occasion of the institution of the Lord's Supper, Jesus said, 'I will not drink of this fruit of the vine from now on until that day when I drink it new with you in my Father's kingdom' (Matt. 26:29). That kingdom is *now*, even though it has *not yet* come to the completion and consummation to be effected when Jesus returns. Surely the fellowship at the Lord's Table is a foretaste and anticipation, in sign and symbol, of the promised 'marriage supper of the Lamb' that will take place in heaven (Rev. 19:7-9). Jesus already communes with believers and will continue to do so while the world lasts.

3. Believers receive grace from Jesus Christ

Why did Jesus institute the Supper? The answer is so that it would be to us a 'cup of blessing' — a cup blessed in itself for what it represents, and therefore designed to be a blessing to those who partake of it. 'The cup of blessing which we bless, is it not the communion of the blood of Christ? The bread which we break, is it not the communion of the body of Christ?' (1 Cor. 10:16). Clearly, the blessing flows from the Lord, in virtue of his atoning death for sinners. He imparts himself, his comfort, his assurance, his love — the very love that took him from eternity to Calvary in the first place. In the Supper, says Samuel Rutherford, speaking of faithfully participating believers, 'Our soul by true faith eats and drinks Christ's flesh and blood, and we are nourished and grow up in him, and our union among ourselves is sealed up.'[3]

Here, then, is what the Lord's Supper is to be to us — a means of grace, a conveyance of divine love to the soul, in imparting of Christ to the renewed heart, a communion of saints with their Saviour.

Visible signs

How is the Lord's Supper a means of grace to believers? In what way, or ways, does the Lord make the connection with us and impart his grace to us? The general answer is that he accomplishes this through *visible signs* that represent the realities of invisible grace.

The visible signs have no power in themselves

Human nature seems perennially addicted to venerating its traditions, myths, relics and symbols. From science fiction to religion, the attraction of the magical appears irresistible. Titles like 'Holy Land' (Israel), 'Holy Places' (Jerusalem, etc.) and 'Holy Father' (the pope), for example, all conjure up an aura of the immediate and miraculous presence of the divine in places and a person, and yet are, from a biblical perspective, entirely bogus. Yet they excite millions, shape politics and cause wars.

In the case of the Holy Supper, as the Lord's Supper is often quite properly called, the holiness does not reside in some grace operating in the substance of the bread and wine. Still less is there some automatic conveyance of grace to any and all who partake of it, in virtue of the mere administration of the correct form of the sacrament. There is no 'miracle of the mass', in which the bread becomes flesh at the tinkling of the bell and utterance of the priest's *'Hoc est corpus meum'* ('This is my body'). That is magic, not miracle. And it was not what Jesus did when he first spoke these wonderful words. Jesus was still the whole

Jesus and the bread he gave to the disciples was still bread. 'Is the bread and the wine turned over and changed into Christ's body and blood?' asks Samuel Rutherford. He answers, 'They are changed in their use as being, after they are consecrated by prayer, no longer common food, but in substance and nature they remain bread and wine.' What did Jesus mean by these words? Rutherford again answers: '... because as truly as we eat and drink in faith, as truly we receive Christ crucified and all his blessings and are spiritually nourished in him... He meant, "This bread which I have taken, blessed, and broken (1 Cor. 10:16; Acts 20:7; 1 Cor. 11), is a sacrament and pledge that I do surely give to you believers my body and blood to be food to nourish your souls," as when a lord delivers to a captain the keys of his castle, he says, "Behold, I give you my house to keep."'[4]

The efficacy of the Lord's Supper is not in the elements of bread and wine themselves, nor in the mere utterance of the words of institution, as if the former were touchstones of some kind and the latter a wonder-working spell. Mere physical presence, including hearing the words and ingesting the elements, does not secure some portion of grace. The power of the Supper is in the presence of Christ working by the Holy Spirit in the hearts of believing participants who receive the symbols in faith, according to the Word of God. The transaction is no less wonderful, or supernatural, for being spiritual in nature, as opposed to being physically — and crassly — magical, as in the case of Rome's transubstantiation myth.

The visible signs are symbolic of Christ's death

The bread and wine, then, are symbols of Christ's flesh and blood. Sacramental use of these elements is a holy use of ordinary things, and as such is to be conducted with the utmost reverence. Why? Because these symbols speak of Christ's provision of redemption for his people. Here is how it unfolds in the course of the Supper:

1. *Setting apart the elements with prayer* — as the Lord did (1 Cor. 11:24) — speaks of the setting apart of our Lord from all eternity to take our flesh, and assume the office of Mediator between God and man.

2. *Breaking the bread* before giving it to the disciples — as the Lord did (11:24) — provides a vivid picture of the brokenness of his body on the cross and reminds us that, while death is the penalty for sin, his death is the sufficient payment for the sins of others.

3. *Pouring the wine* — to put it in the cup (11:25) — evokes the awful spectacle of the shedding of blood through the piercing of his hands and feet and side, and correspondingly elevates the intensity of his sacrifice for sin. 'Without shedding of blood, there is no remission' of sin (Heb. 9:22).

4. *Eating the bread and drinking the wine* indicate both his gracious provision of salvation and our believing reception of that provision, and represent also the continuing

promise of the Lord to be 'the author and finisher of our faith' (Heb. 12:2).

5. *Eating and drinking together at the Lord's Table* emphasizes that believers are part of a fellowship with Christ and in Christ. The church, as instituted according to Christ's revealed will, administers and celebrates the very character of the body of Christ as a redeemed people.[5] We are neither to invent our own church and ministry — as did Micah in the days of the judges of Israel and Jeroboam after the secession of the ten tribes (Judg. 17:1-13; 1 Kings 12:31; 13:2) — nor to stay aloof from a true church of Jesus Christ. No individual may make himself his own church and serve himself with his own sacrament. Christ gave the Lord's Supper to the church as his body, visible, gathered and ordered, with a sound ministry and a believing membership.

6. *The word of Christ* precedes and accompanies the administration of the symbols of his sacrificial death, and together these declare afresh the will of Christ for our lives. It is the Word of God preached that sets the context for the Supper and prepares the hearts of the communicants for spiritual communion with Christ. God's Word teaches us the gospel that is given visual expression in the actions and elements of the sacrament. The Word teaches us to look back and to look forward at the same time. We behold the cross and ponder the emptiness of the tomb. We await the coming of the risen Christ and look to his present intercession and heavenly rule on our behalf (Heb. 7:25; Eph. 1:22). We give thanks for his death as that which secured

heaven for believers, and for his life as that which guarantees the progress of the church in this world until he comes at the end of the age.

The visible signs are seals of God's promise

A sign is only a sign because it can be seen. Signs are tangible things. The elements of bread and wine are visible *signs*, which, when received in the act of a living faith in Christ, are then *seals* upon the believer of the promise of God to save those for whom Jesus died and rose again (Rom. 4:25). The relationship of sign and seal is beautifully expounded by Paul when he shows that Abraham had received 'the sign of circumcision' and that it was also 'a seal of the righteousness of the faith which he had while still uncircumcised' (Rom. 4:11). It was a seal of something deeper than the sign itself.

A seal *pledges* the validity and certainty of the thing signified. It is a mark of authority and a stamp of authenticity. That is why we have such elaborate arrangements for such things in daily life as receipts and affidavits, certificates and diplomas. These are inanimate extensions of the biblical requirement for multiple witnesses to the commitments they represent. They seal the integrity of those who 'sign on the dotted line'. Similarly, the symbols of the Lord's Supper — bread and wine — are pledges of the validity of Christ's death as an atonement for sin and the certainty of his purpose of salvation for all who will believe in him. They are, observes Herman Hoeksema, 'as it were, the oath of God, which He will surely fulfil'.[6]

A seal likewise *proclaims* that the one who gives the seal takes ownership and responsibility for what the sign sets apart. In the Old Testament, circumcision and the Passover both declared that Israel belonged to God. In the New Testament, baptism and the Lord's Supper set apart the new 'Israel of God' as the people of God's own possession (Gal. 6:16).

A seal also *presupposes* something in the person to whom the sign is given. For example, the seal on a university degree diploma not only pledges the validity of the degree conferred, but also presupposes that the graduate has indeed fulfilled his commitments. As we have seen, Abraham received 'the sign of circumcision', which was also 'a seal of the righteousness of the faith which he had while still uncircumcised...' (Rom. 4:11). So the signs of bread and wine are also seals of faith already professed by those who come to communion. In coming to the Supper, communicants both profess faith and are confirmed in their faith. On the other hand, communing will do nothing for the unbeliever who dares to come forward except incur greater guilt and judgement, for he is in the condition of 'not discerning the Lord's body' (1 Cor. 11:27,29).

Finally, a seal *presages* the potential usefulness of what it seals for those who do not yet possess it themselves. Participation in the Lord's Supper is only for confessing Christian believers. But its very existence in the life of the church challenges those who have not, and may not yet, come to the Supper to come to Christ, to the crucified, dead, buried and risen Saviour, that they too may have everlasting life and, having confessed Christ before men

(Matt. 10:32), may be welcomed to proclaim his death at the Lord's Table.

The Lord's Supper conveys the grace of Jesus Christ to believers as they faithfully participate. From Jesus' standpoint, it is a sign and seal to believers of the efficacy of his atonement for their sin. From the believer's standpoint, it is the proclamation of the Lord's death — both a profession of faith from the heart, and a confirmation of faith to the heart. Over two centuries ago, a Scottish denomination called the Associate Presbytery ('the Seceders') published a catechism on the Westminster Assembly's *Shorter Catechism.* This excellent work, called *Fisher's Catechism* after one of its editors, James Fisher, beautifully explains and applies the point we have been discussing. These are all in explanation of question 96 in the *Shorter Catechism.*

> *Question 29:* What is it to show forth the death of Christ?
>
> *Answer:* It is to profess [by partaking of this sacrament], that we believe his death, in our room [place, GJK], to have been most acceptable to God (Eph. 5:2); and that we acquiesce therein, together with his obedience, is the sole ground of our hope of salvation (Rom. 4:25).

> *Question 33:* What is it about the death of Christ we ought to remember in the sacrament?
>
> *Answer:* The truth of it: the necessity of it; and the sufficiency of it.

Question 34: What is it to remember the truth of Christ's death?

Answer: It is by a true and saving faith, to believe that Christ really did and suffered all these things for us, that are recorded of him in Scripture (1 Cor. 15:3-4).

Question 35: What is it to remember the necessity of his death? (Luke 24:26: 'Ought not Christ to have suffered these things?')

Answer: It is to believe, that we had certainly gone down to the pit, unless God had found a ransom, or an atonement (Job 33:24).

Question 36: What is it to remember the sufficiency of it?

Answer: It is to believe that it is *infinitely valuable*: and therefore could have secured the salvation of *thousands* of worlds, had it been so ordained, it being the death and blood of him, who is the supreme God (Acts 20:28: 'Feed the church of God, which he hath purchased with his own blood.')

The visible signs speak of Christ's death. They constantly bring us back to the foot of the cross, to the ground of our salvation. They call us to proclaim the victory of the risen Saviour over death and the grave, to the end that we might grow in grace and that the world might hear the gospel of saving grace in Jesus Christ, Son of God and Saviour of the world.

3.
The presence of Christ

'Take, eat; this is my body which is broken for you; do this in remembrance of me... This cup is the new covenant in my blood. This do, as often as you drink it, in remembrance of me' (1 Cor. 11:24-25).

The Christian thirsts for the nearness of Christ. This should not be difficult to understand. We know what it is to be close to our loved ones. That is why families gather at festive times of the year and for birthdays and anniversaries. A sense of closeness, and of connection, deepens and strengthens natural bonds and relationships. So it is with Christ, for every believer.

Jesus' great name, Immanuel (literally, 'God with us'), asserts his determination to be with his people (Matt. 1:23). This was established in the incarnation. Through his birth to Mary, God the Son took human nature, and assumed our flesh. He lived among us and 'was in all points tempted as we are, yet without sin' (Heb. 4:15). He 'learned obedience by the things which he suffered' (Heb. 5:8). He was obedient to the point of death, even the death on a cross (Phil. 2:8).

Even in the face of his bodily departure, he affirmed his determination to be with his people. He did so in terms of his promise to send the Holy Spirit to be the indwelling Helper of believers in this life (John 14:26; 15:26; 16:13). And with respect to the next life, he proclaimed the prospect of the hope of heaven and his bodily return (Matt. 28:20; 1 Thess. 4:17).

This is also signified and sealed in the Lord's Supper, for, as we saw in the last chapter, the essence of the Supper is that he comes to commune with us and nourishes us inwardly in the act of faithful participation. Inevitably, the question arises as to how, and in what way, Christ is present with us in the Supper. He is, after all, in heaven, in his resurrection body, ruling as King of kings at the right hand of the Father's majesty (Heb. 1:3,13; 8:1; 10:12; 12:2; 1 Peter 3:22). How, then, does he presence himself with his people, as in a myriad of places around the world they come to the Table and commune with their Saviour? Is there a real presence of Christ in these often simultaneous celebrations?

In answering these questions, we should note that Jesus is always with his people spiritually, constantly feeds his people spiritually and, in the Lord's Supper, communes with his people spiritually.

Jesus is always with his people spiritually

It is important for our encouragement and comfort to be clear that Jesus is really and objectively present with believers at all times. This is true even when, subjectively, we may feel left alone, perhaps by reason of doubt, sin, or even things as mundane as sickness or tiredness.

This is more than a general omnipresence of Christ in his divine nature

God is omnipresent to all people throughout all time and space, whether they are believers or unbelievers. God is *immanent* in his creation. He never slumbers or sleeps (Ps. 121:4). His eyes are constantly upon the righteous and his face is against those who do evil (1 Peter 3:12). He warns us clearly that 'There is no creature hidden from his sight, but all things are naked and open to the eyes of him to whom we must give account' (Heb. 4:13). He is present in the preaching of the Word as it searches the thoughts and intents of our hearts (Heb. 4:12).

The Son of God is present with his people in a distinctly personal way. This is a loving, gracious, caring, guiding presence, in which he acts as the believer's interface with God as a heavenly Father, in terms of his being the accepted sacrifice for their sin that reconciles them to God. He has told the church in the world, 'And lo, I am with you always, even to the end of the age' (Matt. 28:20). That is, in every situation and circumstance, both collectively (i.e., the church as the temple of God and the body of Christ, 1 Cor. 3:16; 12:27) and individually (i.e., each believer as a temple of the Holy Spirit, 1 Cor. 6:19), he is truly and constantly our Immanuel.

Jesus is spiritually, not bodily, present with us

Jesus is obviously not with us bodily. Since his ascension, he is represented to us in Scripture as enthroned in heaven, in his resurrection body, at the right hand of the Majesty on high (Heb. 1:3). Many Christians think of Jesus as a kind of wraith that courses about the world to minister to people. He is, however, not a spirit. He is still, and for ever, the God-man, the incarnate Son — six feet or so of glorified human body, physically present in that one place in heaven! The projection of his real presence elsewhere is not accomplished by miraculous perambulations around the universe in his body, or by an omnipresent extension of his divine nature, but *by the Holy Spirit*, whom he has sent to be the 'Helper' of his people (John 14:16,26; 15:26; 16:7). He is present spiritually, by the Spirit he has sent. His presence is not a figment of our imagination, or some epiphenomenon of pious thoughts — that is, it is not a psychological state essentially generated by us. His is a real, objective presence, to which believers are made sensitive by faith, as the Holy Spirit operates within their hearts.

A heart changed and renewed by the gospel knows and sees the presence of Jesus with the eyes of understanding. The same Holy Spirit who regenerates human nature and converts sinners to Christ perfectly represents Christ in their lives. By the Holy Spirit, Christ is always with his people as surely as if he were physically present with us.

Jesus constantly feeds his people spiritually

It is important to remember that Jesus not only feeds his people spiritually by means of the Lord's Supper, but does so constantly through the other means of grace. He teaches this very clearly in his 'bread of life' sermon (John 6:22-59).

In this passage, we are commanded to feed on Christ. There is no reference here to the Lord's Supper, but rather to believing, trusting and laying hold of Christ in the exercise of personal faith. We feed on him as the bread of life by believing in him, receiving the truth of his Word, loving him and keeping his commandments as his disciples, and rejoicing unto eternal life. 'Most assuredly,' says Jesus, 'unless you eat the flesh of the Son of Man and drink his blood, you have no life in you' (John 6:53). 'It is the Spirit who gives life; the flesh profits nothing. The words that I speak to you are spirit, and they are life' (John 6:63). 'Man shall not live by bread alone, but by every word that proceeds from the mouth of God' (Matt. 4:4, quoting Deut. 8:3).

Eating the 'flesh' and drinking the 'blood' of Jesus are obviously figurative and not literal. These terms refer to being one with Christ in his death, receiving him in terms of his giving of himself as the sacrifice for sin. We feed on him spiritually as the sin-bearer who atoned for our sins through death on the cross. Jesus is with his people constantly. He feeds them constantly. He does these things quite apart from the Lord's Supper. But it is in the Holy Supper that they come together in a particularly vivid way.

Jesus communes with his people spiritually

In the Supper, the spiritual feeding on Christ and the sense of his presence are accompanied and stimulated by eating and drinking the visible symbols of his atoning death as our substitute. And there is a real, though spiritual, connection between the *signs* and the *thing signified*, so that our faith is strengthened as Christ communicates of himself to the believing communicant.

How is Jesus present?

Jesus says, 'This is my body... This cup is the new covenant in my blood.' Does this mean that Jesus *is*, or *becomes*, the bread and wine (as the Roman Catholic doctrine of transubstantiation teaches)? Or does it mean that Jesus is somehow *'in, under, and along with'* with the elements, even if they still look, feel and taste like bread and wine (as the Lutheran doctrine of consubstantiation claims)? If neither of these is true, what does Jesus mean by 'This is my body'?

1. Jesus is spiritually present

We must say that the bread and wine are no more literally the flesh and blood of Jesus than he is literally a 'vine', or a 'door' (John 15:1; 10:9). The Bible is full of figurative expressions that vividly illumine the person and the mission of Christ. Philip Henry (1631-97), the father of the famous commentator Matthew Henry, published a lovely book in 1691 from his own sermons on Christ as he is presented to us in Scripture under no fewer than thirty-nine such figurative expressions![1] He is the fountain, the door, the dew, and so on. There is, of course, a reality behind each of these figures or symbols, but it cannot, and must not, be reduced to the thing itself in a literal sense.

We must therefore reject any idea that the Lord is spatially present *in* the elements (transubstantiation) or *with* the elements (consubstantiation). The concept of transubstantiation reaches back to the work of Radbertus of Corbie in the ninth century, although the standard formulation of this teaching comes from Hildebert of Tours around A.D. 1134. But it was Lanfranc, Archbishop of Canterbury from A.D. 1070-89, who made the most celebrated remark with reference to the mass, when he wrote, 'The very body of Christ was truly held in the priest's hand, broken and chewed by the teeth of the faithful.' This is mystical sleight of hand, not sound exegesis. It also has the effect of rendering the sacrament into a repeated sacrifice of Christ, when in fact the Supper is supposed to be a celebration of the once-for-all satisfaction which his death accomplished at the time. In Jesus' own words of institution, his reference to his blood — 'this cup' — is obviously figurative. No one has ever advocated the transubstantiation of the cup! The notion that he was making the bread in his hands and the wine in the cup into extra-corporeal pieces of his flesh is without any foundation in the exegesis of the relevant texts. The sacramental bread and wine died for nobody. It was Christ's body that was nailed to the cross — the same body that is now risen and enthroned in glory at the right hand of God's majesty. The bread and wine are only the symbols of the body that was broken and the blood that was shed.

2. Jesus is present to believers

What is happening in connection with the bread and wine in the Supper is that Christ is really present, spiritually and personally to believers in the faithful administration and reception of the sacrament. Thus Charles Hodge observes, 'He who in faith receives the cup, receives the covenant of which it was the pledge; and he who receives in faith the bread receives the benefits of Christ's body as broken for sin. The one is the symbol and pledge of the other.'[2]

What does this teach us about our coming to the Table?

There is nothing more miserable in the life of the church than a cold, dead use of the means of grace. When preaching becomes no more than 'the talk' and, instead of proclaiming Christ and him crucified, the focus is baptized sociology, we know that 'Ichabod' ('The glory has departed,' 1 Sam. 4:20-21) is written over the portals of what used to be a real church. Similarly, when people will come to communion but live the rest of the time as if God is dead, you know that the church is under judgement.

A sound doctrine of the Lord's Supper has far-reaching practical implications for the way in which we come to the Table and go from it to live for Jesus.

1. It is a profoundly spiritual exercise

We must grasp that this is to be no mere ritual, but a solemn and vital act of faith in which God in Christ is present to work in us both to will and to do of his good pleasure.

There is a spiritual *food* for the soul. Christ is the true meat and drink that endures for ever (John 6:35).

There is a spiritual *work* in heart and mind. The Holy Spirit sent by Christ is imparted in fresh measure to believers (John 14:17).

There is a spiritual *mouth* to receive the bread of life. Faith is the medium by which Christ is both received and proclaimed as the only Saviour of sinners (Gal. 3:14).

2. It is a blessed exercise

We are to come believing and expecting blessing. We come in order to meet with Christ, to confess Christ, to grow in the grace of Christ, and all on the basis of his promise to give of himself to us. It is a 'cup of blessing which we bless', says Paul (1 Cor. 10:16). Jesus is really present and calls us to focus upon his death and his victory over sin and the grave. It is as if his whole being and ministry are telescoped into this one sacrament. From virgin birth to earthly life and ministry, to death, to resurrection, to heavenly rule, to bodily return, the incarnate Son meets us at his Supper. The heart of the gospel is laid out in symbol on the Lord's Table: our need, and his provision; our response and his assurance; our hope and his promise. Although in taking the symbols of the dying Jesus we proclaim his death, we actually extol his life and declare him to be the life-giver. We actually receive the life he gives. In the midst of death, we see life. We look at the cross, and see the plains of heaven and rejoice with joy unspeakable and full of glory.

3. It is a mandatory exercise

If we know the Lord at all, we must come. To be sure, Christ presences himself with us in other contexts and at other times. He comes to us in all the public and private means of grace — the word, the sacrament and prayer. He never leaves his own dear people (Ps. 139:7-8; cf. Mal. 3:16).

In the Lord's Supper, however, he communes with us in this special action of a symbolic meal, conducted before heaven and the world. The focus is not upon whatever may have been the doctrine of the Word read and preached on the given day. Neither is it on the current circumstances of our lives and the state of the world. Nor is it even on the specific needs of the moment that press in upon us and lead us to cry to God in secret prayer for his help. The focus in the Supper is invariably, exclusively, pervasively and magisterially upon the heart of the gospel. It therefore encompasses the atoning death he died on the cross, the sufficiency of his sacrifice for sin and our need of a Saviour. This in turn brings before us our relationship to him, and our personal knowledge of him as our Saviour, his coming to us as the crucified and risen Christ, his covenant and promise, his gift of redemption and eternal life, and his coming again to take his people to glory.

In the Lord's Supper, Jesus' presence is rendered so palpably personal that at the Table we must profess him from the heart as our Saviour and respond in faith by laying hold upon him afresh as our Lord. The Lord's Supper faithfully administered does not allow the communicants to sit back and admire the proceedings with detachment in the way people sometimes admire a piece of pageantry or even an elegant point in a sermon. Neither does it allow us to go out from ourselves to others in saying 'Amen' to a request in a prayer, as if we are only spectators of other people's needs and have none of our own. In the Supper, we face Jesus and he confronts us. This happens in a unique way, because the symbols of his broken body and shed blood bring Christ our substitute to our souls and call us to embrace him with wholehearted commitment and unalloyed joy. To remain distant from him, in the face of such vivid and immediate directness, we must want to fob him off. We must choose to be cool and decide to be detached. God forbid that this should ever be so! Rather let us embrace the Saviour while he is near.

4.
Proclaiming the Lord's death

'For as often as you eat this bread and drink this cup, you proclaim the Lord's death till he comes' (1 Cor. 11:26).

The idea of memorials for the dead is to keep their memories alive. The Cenotaph in London, the Arc de Triomphe in Paris, the Vietnam Memorial in Washington, and places such as the Gettysburg battlefield and the Normandy beaches are powerful testimonies that the dead do matter. What they did matters — matters to us who follow after, and so lives on in our lives.

This is all the more true of the memorials in our hearts of departed loved ones and friends. Sorrowing for their passing is mingled with joy for what they meant to us. They too, infinitely more personally, still live in our lives. Writing in 1863, the Scottish preacher Henry Belfrage tied this in to the Lord's Supper when he observed, 'A departed friend has claims on our remembrance, in proportion to the excellencies of his character, and to the services he has done us. Such a friend is often present to our thoughts; but when the day returns, on which he bestowed upon us some signal marks of his affection, or in which he subjected himself for our sake to danger or suffering ... the heart impels us at such seasons to go to his grave to weep there; and we bless his memory with encomiums of gratitude and love. And shall we be thus to earthly friends, and forget our best Friend?'[1]

In the Lord's Supper, the apostle Paul tells us, we 'proclaim the Lord's death till he comes' — that is, as long as the world lasts, and in prospect of Jesus' coming again at the end of the age. We proclaim the death that gave us life. We proclaim the Saviour who rose from the grave, having conquered sin and death, in order to give everlasting life to all who would believe in him.

The great question here is, of course, 'What does it mean to proclaim Christ's death in this way?' We may best answer this by dividing the question. First, what does the Lord's Supper teach us about Christ's death? Secondly, what does it mean to proclaim Christ's death at the Lord's Table?

What does the Lord's Supper teach us about Christ's death?

The Lord's Supper shows us that dying for sinners was the great work that Jesus came to do as the *Saviour* of sinners. Neither his birth nor his earthly ministry would have come to anything had he not submitted to death on the cross. The manner of his going seals the import of his coming. Important as his incarnation is, it is Jesus' atoning death that actually secures redemption for lost people. Bethlehem is the opening shot, but Calvary is the final battle. This is why the Lord's Supper is the one and only feast given in the New Testament commanded to be observed regularly by the church. Here, the heart of the gospel is distilled to its finest essence, as nowhere else in the life of God's people.

It is possible to profess love for the 'babe in the manger' of the Christmas carols, or to admit an appreciation for the great teacher of the 'Sermon on the Mount', while at the same time doubting or rejecting outright the very idea of redemption through the shedding of the blood of Christ. It is surely obvious, however, that to claim to be a follower of Jesus and yet be offended by the cross is tantamount to denying him altogether. Whatever genuflection may be made to the moral teaching and example of the Saviour, setting aside his death, as the necessary sacrifice for sin and condition for salvation, is to set aside the Christian gospel and the Lord himself. Jesus calls believers to proclaim his death, precisely because it is that death that brings them to saving faith, newness of life and the promise of heaven. 'For where there is a testament, there must also of necessity be the death of the testator,' and 'So Christ was offered once to bear the sins of many. To those who eagerly wait for him he will appear a second time' (Heb. 9:16,28).

A violent death

The Lord's Supper shows us the *way* Jesus died. Perhaps it is too obvious to remark that Jesus did not die in his bed. Crucifixion was a slow agony, designed to torture as it killed. The bread broken and the wine poured out tell of violent death. His wrists and ankles were smashed by the nails. His side was pierced by a spear thrust. His back had been torn and bloodied by the *verberatio* — the application of a terrible scourge made up of multiple thongs inset with shards of lead and bone. From the human side, this was judicial murder, but in the plan of God, it achieved the salvation of the world.

The words, 'They ... crucified the Lord of glory' (1 Cor. 2:8) can so easily slide across the mind and mask the awful agonies of Christ, the greatest of which must have been the righteous anger of the Father. Jesus went through hell that afternoon and died under the burden of the sin from which he was determined to save the people who would fill the streets of heaven. 'For he made him who knew no sin to be sin for us, that we might become the righteousness of God in him' (2 Cor. 5:21). Christ accepted the 'wages of sin' — the sin of others — that, in believing, we might receive his righteousness to our account. There is a double substitution in the death of Christ: our sin for his sinlessness and his righteousness for our unrighteousness. He is forsaken by his Father under the punishment of our sin, and we are reconciled to the Father on account of the imputation of his righteousness. That is why those who love Christ Jesus can exultantly confess with Charles Wesley:

He breaks the power of cancelled sin,
He sets the prisoner free;
His blood can make the foulest clean,
His blood availed for me.

A sacrificial death

The Lord's Supper shows us Jesus as the *sacrifice* for sin. The symbols of bread and wine visibly represent Christ's giving of himself as the one and only and sufficient sacrifice for sin. Whatever the Jewish leadership and Pontius Pilate thought they were doing, God was in fact laying the sins of sinners on his only begotten Son and Jesus, for his part, was willingly bearing the righteous justice of God against sin as the substitute for all who would believe in him. In this way, Jesus both *propitiates* God's offended holiness and *expiates* our guilt, so removing God's righteous condemnation of us and securing our pardon, justification and newness of life. This is the very heart of the Supper, for had Christ not given himself to the cross as a substitutionary sacrifice for sin, there would be no ground whatsoever for our salvation. Every time we eat that bread and drink of that cup, we are reminded that, outside of Christ, it is our body and blood that would be required as the penalty for our personal sin and unrighteousness.

Furthermore, neither Christ nor the cross came out of the blue into what we call the first century. Christ was born, lived among us, died, rose again, ascended into heaven and will come again on the last great day of the history of this present world, all in fulfilment of very long-standing prophecies and promises of the Old Testament Scriptures. You will frequently hear talk of Jesus as 'the founder of the Christian religion', as if he were just one of a number of influential men in history who started religions of their own and managed to gather something of a following. That, however, promotes and perpetuates a fundamental misunderstanding of the plan and purpose of God as revealed in his Word. From the beginning, God planned to save a human race that had fallen, in Adam, into the condition of alienation from God that the Bible calls sin and condemnation (John 3:18-19; Rom. 3:23; 5:12).

As early as Genesis 3, the so-called *protevangelium* (i.e., 'proto-gospel') promises that one day the 'Seed' of the woman — the Redeemer God would provide — would bruise 'the head' of the serpent — sin and condemnation as the work of the world, the flesh and the devil. In the process of vanquishing sin, death and Satan, this Son of Man would suffer the bruising of his 'heel', clearly a reference to his sufferings in that once-for-all struggle (Gen. 3:15). The sacrifices, ceremonies and priesthood of the Old Testament continued to point to the promise of a Saviour whose sacrifice of himself would atone for sin.

This cannot be expounded here, but the laws of sacrifice, from the Passover in Egypt to the tabernacle in the wilderness (esp. Exod. 12-13; Lev. 1-7), the prophecies of the Messiah in the Psalms (esp. Ps. 2; 8; 22; 69; 110; 118) and the Prophets (esp. Isa. 7; 9; 40-43; 49-53; Micah 5:2-4; Zech. 13-14; Mal. 3:1-7) and the reflection on their fulfilment in Christ as the great High Priest in the Epistle to the Hebrews — all combine to establish the fact that the 'Seed' of the woman and of Abraham is Christ (Gal. 3:16). From eternity, God decreed the redemption of a people to himself through the Christ (Eph. 1:3-6).

At the Lord's Table, Christians receive the visible tokens of this wonderful work of the God who 'is love', and who so loved the world he had made that 'He gave his only begotten Son, that whoever believes in him should not perish but have everlasting life' (1 John 4:8; John 3:16).

A covenantal death

The Lord's Supper shows Jesus to be our *covenant head.* Jesus died as the representative of his people. 'For as in Adam all die, even so in Christ shall all be made alive' (1 Cor. 15:22). Jesus died and rose from the dead as the 'Mediator of a better covenant' (Heb. 8:6). He bore the punishment and rose incorruptible from the dead on the third day. Therefore, all who are united to him in faith will be forgiven and cleansed, and also will be raised incorruptible (1 Cor. 15:52-53). 'In this ordinance therefore,' says Charles Hodge, 'Christ is set forth as a sacrifice which at once makes expiation for sin and ratifies the covenant of grace.'[2]

The Supper is, therefore, a covenant meal, in which the shared bond of union with Christ is celebrated by the Lord's people as they remember and proclaim his death as the source of their new life. Heaven itself is called 'the marriage supper of the Lamb', in virtue of the consummation of Christ's covenant love for his people — a consummation in which all the redeemed rejoice together and for ever in their risen Saviour (Rev. 19:9).

A conquering death

The Lord's Supper declares that Christ's death is a death to be proclaimed 'till he comes'. His death is proclaimed because he is alive and is coming again. Believers celebrate

Christ as the one whose death actually killed death. He rose from the dead on the third day. He will come again at the end of the age. He will gather together all whom he saves and will judge the living and the dead. He will consummate his kingdom, that kingdom over which he now rules from the right hand of the majesty on high, that kingdom which he, on that great day, will have completely subdued and delivered up to his Father (Eph. 1:22; Heb. 1:3; 1 Cor. 15:24).

The Lord's Supper is not a funereal remembrance of a departed loved one, but the exultant anticipation of a returning conqueror. At the Lord's Table believers do not grieve for an absent Lord, but rejoice in the author and finisher of their faith who is both ever present and coming again. He is proclaimed *Christus Victor*, the victorious Christ.

What does it mean for us to proclaim Christ's death at the Lord's Table?

The great question with all statements of biblical truth is how they ought to interact with our experience. It is possible to come to the Lord's Supper with a certain theological correctness and yet be coldly detached from that teaching. It is one thing, then, to understand in some formal sense what the Lord's Supper teaches about Jesus' death. It is something else again to proclaim that truth with the conviction of a heart warmed by his free grace and moved to eternal gratitude by his sacrifice for one so unworthy as oneself. We therefore need to be quite clear as to what it means in Christian experience to proclaim his death and what every observance of the sacrament is designed to produce in the movements of the soul.

Inwardly

Inwardly, we must review afresh our relationship to the Lord, recommit our way to him, and rejoice in his precious salvation. The Supper, every time it is observed, is properly the occasion of comprehensive personal review and evaluation — and, if need be, a fresh start in personal discipleship to Christ.

The leading questions for reflection are surely, 'Why was it necessary for Jesus to die — to die for *me*, to die in *my place*?' and, 'What are the implications of his death *for my life*?'

1. We must grieve over our sin

Not just sins in particular, but sin itself as an underlying feature of our thought life and actual performance. Sin in the heart precedes sinfulness of the hands. This is true in Christians, even though it is true that the believer is free from the law of sin and death. Christ is the believer's Lord, but Christians still stumble in many things (James 3:2). Think of the ways we shame our Saviour. We constantly need a sense of our sin, a discernment of our failings and a spirit of repentance — that 'godly sorrow' that 'produces repentance leading to salvation, not to be regretted', as opposed to the 'sorrow of the world' that 'produces death'

(2 Cor. 7:10). You see, it was *our sin* that took Jesus to the cross, to the end that he would cancel it out and save us from our sins. 'We best remember Christ crucified,' says Thomas Manton, 'when we are crucified with him: Gal. 2:20, "I am crucified with Christ"; when the sensual inclination is mortified, and the heart deadened to the pleasures of sin, which are but for a season.'[3] This is not morbidity or negativism, as some today would have us think, but a straightforward and serious consideration of the relationship between Jesus' death and my life, to the end that I love him by keeping his commandments, with holy intelligence and godly enthusiasm.

2. We must rejoice in Christ

If sorrow focuses on sin, faith focuses on the Saviour who gives us new life. We will rejoice, must rejoice, and can only rejoice, if we believe that his death is available for our deliverance, and we are actively trusting in his death for our own salvation. There is both knowledge of truth as it is in Jesus, and trust in the Jesus who is the truth (and the way, and the life, John 14:6).

Then the Lord's Supper is truly for us a feast and not a fast. The 'bridegroom' is with us in a special and personal way (cf. Mark 2:19). Tears of repentance speedily give way to tears of joy. 'We also rejoice in God,' says Paul, 'through our Lord Jesus Christ, through whom we have now received the reconciliation' (Rom. 5:11). Speaking prophetically of the saving work of the promised Messiah, the psalmist lays the ground of the joy of the redeemed:

> The poor shall eat and be satisfied;
> Those who seek him will praise the LORD.
> Let your heart live for ever!
>
> (Ps. 22:26).

When the Messiah did come, he affirmed this same truth in the most exalted and luminous terms: 'For God so loved the world that he gave his only begotten Son, that whoever believes in him should not perish but have everlasting life' (John 3:16). Where, in this world and in the Christian life, should there be more rejoicing for those whom Jesus has saved than at the Lord's Table?

Externally

Externally, we witness to the grace of our Saviour Jesus. A faith that lies hidden in the heart is instantly suspect. Faith without works is dead — that is, is not saving faith at all because it is false faith, 'faith by itself' (James 2:17). In complete contrast to this, a heart for God cannot but burst out into practical praise of the Lord who saves his people. These things are felt, if they are real at all.

1. We bless God as our Father

'Blessed be the God and Father of our Lord Jesus Christ, who has blessed us with every spiritual blessing in the heavenly places in Christ' (Eph. 1:3). The sense of being adopted as his child, when otherwise we would have been eternally lost, is a palpable reality to the Christian. We are held in the everlasting arms and under the shadow of the divine wings (Ps. 44:3; 77:15; 36:7; 57:1; 63:7). We are held by our right hand — like a toddler walking with a parent — grasped so firmly in his hand that no one can snatch us away from him or from eternal life with him in glory (Ps. 73:23-24; 139:10; John 10:28). 'My Father, who has given them to me,' says Jesus, 'is greater than all; and no one is able to snatch them out of my Father's hand. I and my Father are one' (John 10:29-30).

2. We are not ashamed, before others, of the gospel of Jesus Christ

Only shame stands between the believer and a witness to the world in which he moves. Paul was able to preach the gospel because all sinful inhibition was swept away by his own experience of the gospel as 'the power of God to salvation for everyone who believes' (Rom. 1:16). He had come to Christ in faith. He had truly believed. Therefore he was free to declare this same salvation to others. The fact that many who think they are Christians utter hardly a cheep about the Saviour they almost covertly profess suggests a deeper problem than timidity. In contrast, see Stephen, the stones of his enemies already arcing towards his martyr destiny, speaking of Christ with an open face and beholding heaven opened and his Saviour awaiting him. The point is not that we should expect such visions of Jesus, but that we should be able to testify as Stephen did, with a heartfelt abandon to the Lord who abandoned his life to redeem us from eternal death. In the Lord's Supper,

Christians testify before the world. The world may not be physically present, in any considerable number, to observe this testimony. That is true. But it is a mistake to imagine that what churches do is hidden from public notice. The presence of churches in a community is a constant reminder that God has claims upon those who pass by on the other side. The very fact that the Lord's Supper is observed at publicly stated times is a testimony inviting the curiosity of the watching world. The reality is that this is the most vivid of pictures of the heart of the gospel. All this declares to the world, watching or ignoring, that Christ is the only Saviour, and that these folk who come to his table profess to be his and proclaim there is no other.

3. We live, day by day, as the disciples of Jesus Christ

The fact is that much of so-called Christendom has reduced the definition of a 'Christian' to anyone who calls himself one, however devoid his life and thinking may be of hard evidence of a saving knowledge of Jesus Christ. This apostasy, followed by large numbers of careless, unthinking, biblically illiterate and morally indifferent sort-of-churchgoers, and fostered by clerics who fall over themselves to tell their flocks why they need pay no attention to the Word of God, has turned the Lord's Supper into a perfunctory ritual. The sum total of this ritual for many, churches and individuals alike, appears to be — attend communion once a year and you remain a member in good standing, assured of the hope of heaven and a Christian burial! Like an offer in the mail that promises a free gift if you do nothing, 'communion' is 'taken' and God's favour assumed, even if no actual discipleship follows in daily life! It beggars all imagination to think that someone can partake of the symbols of Christ's death and then go straight out the door and live as if there really were no God. But it happens, as they say, 'all the time'. Hypocrisy is, after all, the greatest line of least resistance known to man!

The Lord's Supper, however, is an effective means of grace that calls the communicants to lives of continuing obedience and devotion. 'As often' as we eat the bread and drink the cup, we are impelled and empowered to testify with heart and life to the Lord who has bought us with the price of his own blood. And 'as often', be it noted, is not equivalent to 'as infrequently', or 'whenever you get round to coming to the Table'. Both the church, as a body, and individual Christians should love to proclaim the Lord's death till he comes, and to do so 'often', with joy and thanksgiving. Surely the very contemplation of the cost of the cross of Calvary emblazons across the believing soul the deepest conviction of being a debtor to the mercy of God in Christ and calls forth the unreserved response:

> What shall I render to the LORD
> For all his benefits toward me?
> I will take up the cup of salvation,
> And call upon the name of the LORD.
> I will pay my vows to the LORD
> Now in the presence of his people
> (Ps. 116:12-14).

5. Self-examination

'But let a man examine himself, and so let him eat of the bread and drink of the cup' (1 Cor. 11:28).

From all that we have seen so far, it is surely clear that only professing Christians are invited — no, commanded — to come to the Lord's Table. Underlying this are two great facts. The first is that faith in Jesus Christ, professed before, and approved by, the church, together with a life consistent with that profession, is an essential precondition of participation. The Lord's Supper is a confirming ordinance, and a sign and seal of covenant promises already embraced by communicants who must 'proclaim the Lord's death'. The second is that Jesus is spiritually present in the Supper, so as to bless faithful, believing communicants. The giving of that blessing presupposes and requires spiritual discernment — 'discerning the Lord's body' — in the communicants. Faithful communicants understand the meaning of the sacrament, and profess faith in Christ afresh as they commune.

To say that only Christians are to come to the Table is one thing. It is a truth to be believed and a call to be heeded by all who love the Lord. But what of the *attitude*, the state of heart and soul, in which the Christian is to come and commune? Many of the Corinthians had been coming to the Supper in a disorderly, disrespectful and disgraceful way. Some even came drunk! Others came despising their supposed brothers and sisters in the Lord. Behind this was sheer irreverence for the Lord who had instituted the sacrament in the first place. 'God is a holy and jealous God and greatly to be feared,' wrote Charles Simeon. 'In all our approaches to him we should be filled with awe; but a want of reverence prevails among the generality of mankind; even real Christians manifest it sometimes, and that too even in the most sacred ordinances.'[1]

Paul's concern, then, is not merely to convey some true propositions to our minds, but to challenge our consciences as to the care and devotion with which we come into the presence of God at the Lord's Table. The responsibility is ours: 'Let *a man* examine *himself...*', he says. No one can do this for us, however earnestly others may exhort and challenge us. The pastors and elders, who have responsibility for faithful oversight of the Supper and of those whom they admit to the Table, cannot search the thoughts and intentions of our hearts. It is every individual's duty to search his or her soul before the Lord. To encourage us in this, Paul explains the necessity, the focus and the result of proper self-examination.

The necessity of self-examination

'Let a man examine himself' (1 Cor. 11:28), is not an invitation merely to consider the possibility of doing so. Self-examination is not an option. It is an imperative. Not to do so is to sin and to commit oneself to a careless indifference with respect to the things of God.

A charge to be heeded

Self-examination is an ongoing spiritual exercise for every believer, on every occasion of coming to communion. This is the clear teaching of God's Word. Elsewhere, Paul charges us: 'Examine yourselves as to whether you are in the faith. Test yourselves. Do you not know yourselves, that Jesus Christ is in you?' (2 Cor. 13:5). The emphasis here, as in 1 Corinthians 11:28, is not on whether or not they *are* Christians, but whether or not they are *actively living* as Christians who are heart and hand 'in the faith'. Are they living the Christian life? In other words, it is not the question of assurance of faith that is in view, but living in faith, daily, practically and consistently. The psalmist reflects along this line when he says:

> I have considered the days of old,
> The years of ancient times.
> I call to remembrance my song in the night;
> I meditate within my heart,
> And my spirit makes diligent search
>
> (Ps. 77:5-6).

His question is not, 'Am I a believer?', but 'How am I doing as a believer?' or, putting it another way, 'Am I recognizable as a believer?'

What, then, is the state of your soul? If, as you claim, you are a Christian, how is your love for Christ working out in practice? How consistent is your Christian walk, and your practice of truth, with your Christian profession? Are you strong in the faith? Are you weak? Are you careless? Are you diligent? Are you reaching out? Are you consistent? Are you forsaking sin? Are you growing in grace? Do you love your neighbour? Are you rejoicing in Christ? Are you delighting in God?

A warning to be pondered

An important motive for self-examination before God is that there is a real danger of incurring guilt and judgement through the abuse of the things of God (1 Cor. 11:27,29). We humans are frequently disposed to tolerate sin in the world around us, no doubt out of the desire to have our own transgressions excused. The idea that it is 'a fearful thing to fall into the hands of the living God' seems harsh and forbidding (Heb. 10:31).

So here is one of the great ironies of sin in human beings — it makes us lay claim to being more tolerant than God! Love for sin inevitably leads to the redefinition of much sin as good or, if not exactly good, then not exactly bad either. But God is of purer eyes than to behold iniquity (Hab. 1:13). He defines sin. Sin is not a matter of arbitrary rules, but is at every point the denial of the essential holiness of God. Sin is any lack of conformity to, and transgression of, the law of God. 'Whoever commits sin also commits lawlessness, and sin is lawlessness' (1 John 3:4). That is why 'God is a just judge, and God is angry with the wicked every day' (Ps. 7:11).

God cares about the violation of his perfect holiness. He hears and notes the blasphemies against his name that flood across the face of the earth every day. He no more likes being treated with contempt than we do. God takes sin seriously. It follows that if salvation took the sacrifice of his own Son, then forgiveness will never be secured by ignoring him or treating him lightly. God will by no means clear the guilty and unrepentant by simply winking at their sin, or redefining it as good. So if we approach the Supper thoughtlessly, carelessly, with unrepented sin, abusing the symbols of Jesus' death, we in effect treat Christ lightly, if not even contemptuously. We are not being serious about the cross and reverent towards the Saviour who died for the likes of us so that we could be 'new creation[s]' in Christ (2 Cor. 5:17). Godly candour in self-examination really is a matter of life and death. The English Puritan Thomas Doolittle highlights the seriousness of this matter in a most searching manner when he says, 'I think a man who is not fit to die is not fit to receive [the sacrament]. A man should sit down at the Lord's Table with as great care as he would lie down in his grave. He should be as serious for his soul at this ordinance as he would be upon his dying bed. You should go to the Lord's Table as carefully as if you were going into another world.'[2]

A blessing to be enjoyed

For some people, self-examination is a no-go area. They cannot face too much truth about themselves. It is just too deadly to contemplate. Self-examination, however, is not the same thing as morbid introspection. Even in the normal course of daily life, facing up to reality — both our strengths and our weaknesses — has to be infinitely better than indulging fantasies and living a lie. The little boy who got a Superman outfit one Christmas and imagined that he could fly if he put it on, and then 'flew' out of a second-floor window, quickly discovered the danger of his illusion. Reality, however challenging it may be, is a solid basis for positive action. As a basis for making sound decisions, fantasy about ourselves is a rotten floor waiting to crumble at the first pressure and plunge its trusting dupes to their ruin.

Neither is self-examination to be reduced to a relentlessly negative exercise in internal faultfinding. Self-examination is not the same as self-accusation. Rather, it is the means by which we lay hold all the more firmly on Christ because we review our relationship to him with honesty and discernment, and are encouraged and impelled to commit ourselves to fresh obedience. We are not left with a depressing list of personal failures as much as we are given hope for a growing experience of victory, as we trust ourselves to Christ. There is a blessing to be enjoyed, which we deny, and of which we shall be deprived, if we do not come to the Supper with a living faith in exercise.

This requires that we discern the Lord's body, and reflect upon our relationship to the Lord who bought us with the price of his own death.

The focus of self-examination

The words, 'and so let him eat of that bread' (1 Cor. 11:28), indicate that it is Paul's intention and expectation that believers will engage in heartfelt self-examination and will come to the Table. The focus of this self-examination is participation. It is not designed to keep Christians away, but to impel them to fly to Jesus in the repentant, confiding spirit of a lively faith.

Believers are to come to the Table

This positive perspective must be maintained. Why? Because, observes Charles Simeon, Christians will sometimes be 'kept from the table by a sense of their own unworthiness'. But, as the same writer observes, 'To be unworthy, and to partake unworthily, are very different things: yet if we have partaken unworthily in past times, let us humble ourselves for it; and then we may come again with joy.'[3]

Our unworthiness *in ourselves* ought to be a given. We have no merit of our own to commend us to God. Believers in Christ may, and must, come because Christ commands his blessing for them in the Supper, as they participate in faith. In Christ, by faith, we may indeed 'walk worthy' of our Lord (Col. 1:10; 1 Thess. 2:12), but that worthiness is not our own. It is from the Lord. It is also the gift of God to all who are in Christ — to all who believe and confess him.

Unworthy partaking is inevitable in the case of those who are not believers, i.e., who do not have the worthiness of Christ that is accounted to those who truly believe in him.

Unworthy partaking is, sadly, also possible in believers who are worthy in Christ, on account of justifying faith, but, on the day, are careless, unthinking, or irreverent in the manner of their participation. The Supper is for believers, for believing sinners, but not for unrepentant believing sinners in the grip of sinful attitudes towards the Lord, his people, or anyone else, as they are in the act of coming to the Table.

Not a quest for worthiness...

It is important to be clear that this self-examination is *not* a quest for worthiness, as if somehow to prove to ourselves, and to the Lord, that we are good enough to participate. Self-examination is not designed to measure our worthiness, as much as it is to set our *un*worthiness in the context of the worthiness of Jesus Christ, our substitute and Saviour. Being good enough is not the issue. We shall never be good enough in ourselves, and at our best we shall no doubt be flawed. Believing Jesus, trusting Jesus, looking to Jesus, and coming in the obedience of faith to Jesus *is* the issue.

... But of humbly laying hold on Christ

Christian self-examination focuses on the quality and consistency of our Christian life. The goal is that we should come humbly, thankfully, prayerfully and joyfully to Christ, to be strengthened for all the days ahead and to proclaim him as the one in whom we are trusting for time and for eternity.

On the one hand, this rebukes the tendency towards that kind of cold nominalism that takes for granted that I am doing fine with God, because I have been baptized, go to church now and again and am a generally decent person. For too many, the Lord's Supper is little more than one religious community event among many, special in its own way, to be sure, but distinguished by no particular impact upon their lives.

On the other hand, this also challenges the tendency of some oversensitive souls who hold back because of some struggle with sin, or a general nagging feeling that they are *too* unworthy to come. It says, 'Come, trusting Jesus, repenting, believing, and you will receive his enabling grace. Weep, by all means, but come, believing.'

The result of self-examination

The goal of self-examination is that the believer should 'eat of the bread and drink of the cup' (1 Cor. 11:28). The movement of the text is directed to opening, not closing, the path to the Table. This has in view two main results of biblical self-examination.

Believers will come

It bears repeating to say that self-examination is not designed to see if we are good enough, far less sinless. 'If we say that we have no sin, we deceive ourselves, and the truth is not in us' (1 John 1:8). That is true for us all on this side of eternity. The question is rather, as Herman Hoeksema once put it, 'whether I am *in* the faith, and whether in every respect I am always a fighting saint'. We stand before the mirror of Scripture, as those who are trusting Christ and are committed to him, and say with the psalmist:

> Search me, O God,
> And know my heart;
> Try me, and know my anxieties;
> And see if there is any wicked way in me,
> And lead me in the way everlasting
> (Ps. 139:23-24).

Here is the self-examined believer coming to the Lord in his need and in his hope.

Christ will feed believers

So we come, profoundly aware of the sinfulness of sin and our unworthiness in ourselves of Christ our Saviour, but overwhelmingly persuaded of the truth of the word that 'If we confess our sins, he is faithful and just to forgive us our sin and cleanse us from all unrighteousness' (1 John 1:9). Like the tax gatherer in Luke 18:13, we may cry, 'God, be merciful to me a sinner!' But with Peter we will also testify, 'Him [Jesus] God has exalted to his right hand to be Prince and Saviour, to give repentance to Israel and forgiveness of sins' (Acts 5:31).

As we receive the bread and cup in the exercise of faith, we shall be looking to the sufficiency of Christ's death on the cross for our salvation. Self-examination in the Christian can only lead him to the cross. At the cross, he finds the Saviour who is full of grace; Jesus dying for him, in his place, for his sins; to bring him new life, everlasting life, now and for evermore. In Christ's light, we see light. That light indeed searches the remaining dark corners of the soul and exposes the reserves of ignorance and wilful sin lurking there, but it also dispels the darkness and lights the way to glory. Christ will come to us, and we to him. Christ will commune with us and we with him. Christ will feed us, and we shall grow. Therefore, 'Let a man examine himself, and so let him eat of the bread and drink of the cup.'

6.
Discerning the Lord's body

'For he who eats and drinks in an unworthy manner eats and drinks judgement to himself, not discerning the Lord's body' (1 Cor. 11:29).

Often, the most impressive way to learn how important it is to do something properly is to see the consequences of doing it the wrong way. I was once a boy soldier — a member of the CCF (Combined Cadet Force) of my old school, George Heriot's, in Edinburgh. One fine spring morning in 1958, we set off for a 'field day' on the Pentland Hills, resplendent in full battle-dress, with packs and steel helmets, carrying real Lee-Enfield rifles. 'Britain's last hope!' muttered a sceptic in the ranks. Before we mounted an infantry assault on positions prepared overnight by a section of senior cadets, our Company Sergeant Major warned us about the dangers of the blank .303 cartridges with which we had been issued. He held a rifle a few inches from an empty tin can, pulled the trigger, showed us the hole it blew through the can, and asked us if our flesh was tougher than tin! So off we went up the hill into the face of chattering machine-guns and booming grenades, armed with a healthy respect for even blank ammunition!

God's Word shows us the consequences of sin, not to depress us, but so that we may avoid shipwreck by doing things the right way. There are things to learn from the way the Corinthian Christians conducted themselves at the Lord's Supper. The immediate reason for their need of self-examination before communion was that they had so abused the Supper that they had become, in Paul's words, 'guilty of the body and blood of the Lord' (1 Cor. 11:27). This was displeasing to God, because it effectively denied the very meaning of Christ's death and the purpose of the Supper itself. Instead of putting themselves in the way of God's promised blessings, they had incurred his judgements and covered themselves with guilt. We are told this in order that we should not do likewise. It is important that we take to heart what God teaches here about what it means to 'discern the Lord's body' (11:29), why it was that he chastised the Corinthians (11:30-32), and how we are to approach the Lord's Table (11:33-34).

What is it to 'discern the Lord's body'?

The apostle's charge is quite startling: 'For he who eats and drinks in an unworthy manner eats and drinks judgement to himself, not discerning the Lord's body' (11:29). Notice that there is a positive principle here — we must 'discern the Lord's body' — and an admonitory application consisting of a warning about the consequence of transgressing it.

The positive principle: discerning the Lord's body

The word 'discern' (Greek, *dikrino*) means to separate, in the sense of making proper judgements between what is proper and what is not. In this instance, discerning with respect to the Lord's body means seeing the distinctness of the sacramental use of bread and wine over against their ordinary use in daily life. The Lord's Supper is not just another meal. It is special. It is unique. It has nothing to do with food for the stomach. It has everything to do with food for the soul. It has to do with Jesus Christ, the cross and the resurrection, the gospel and the way of salvation.

The bread and wine as used in the sacrament are symbols of what Christ has done, is doing and will yet do for his people. They are visible signs of the invisible grace that flows from the once-for-all sacrifice of Christ in his death for lost people. Discerning the Lord's body means understanding, in a warm, believing way, what the Lord's Supper symbolizes and teaches, how it is meant to bless faithful communicants, and with what humble, reverent participation and commitment to the Lord it is to be approached.

The admonitory application: eating and drinking judgement

To eat and drink in an unworthy manner is to eat and drink judgement to oneself. This is couched in negative terms, but, as we shall see, with a positive intent.

Perhaps the first question to be addressed is: 'Why is this stated so strongly? Is it not a little thing? Why should God be so serious, so stern?' To answer this, we must reflect on the significance of symbols. For example, think of your country's flag. What does it signify? Is it no more than decorative bunting? If people trample on it, or burn it in the street, what do they mean to convey by their actions? Surely such actions are symbolic means of expressing their disenchantment with the country or the government. The meaning of the gesture depends entirely on the power of the symbol that they dispose of so contemptuously. If they were to burn old curtains in the street, they might be considered strange and a bit of a nuisance, but torching the flag is unmistakably a conscious political act of rebellion against the powers that be.

Examples of symbolic actions are found in Scripture. Belshazzar, the King of Babylon, having sacked Jerusalem and seized the sacred vessels from the temple, sealed his contempt for Israel and her God by using them as drinking vessels for the debauchery in his palace. God's response was to write his sentence on the wall and execute justice: 'That very night Belshazzar, king of the Chaldeans, was slain. And Darius the Mede received the kingdom...' (Dan. 5:30-31). The vessels were more than mere vessels. They were the symbols of God's grace for his people. Belshazzar knew what he was doing. So did God.

Another action, this time involving people as symbols, was Absalom's taking of his father's concubines in full view of the people of Jerusalem (2 Sam. 16:21-22). This was to say, 'I am now king in place of David, and there will be no turning back.' We know what the judgements of God were upon that little piece of bombast.

The abuse of the Lord's Supper is more than the careless handling of some food and drink. It is more than accidentally spilling your plate on the floor. It says something about how much, or how little, you really care about Jesus and the things of God.

The *wilful* mockery of the Supper — which reaches beyond the problem of carelessness in Corinth — would, by analogy, incur the guilt of Christ's enemies in their *murdering* Jesus ('betrayers and murderers,' Stephen calls them in Acts 7:52). This is the great unrepented sin of the lost in hell, the reprobate who crucify afresh the Son of God (Heb. 6:6), who were prepared to say, not knowing what they were really saying, 'His blood be on us and on our children' (Matt. 27:25).

The Corinthians did not view themselves as mockers of Christ. They were, however, in effect mocking Christ, even though they thought themselves sincere Christians. They were thoughtless and shallow. They needed to rethink what they were doing, repent and return to intelligent obedience across the whole spectrum of their lives as believers. They needed to see that staggering up to the Lord's Table in a drunken state, or coming forward with resentment in their hearts towards their brothers and sisters in Christ, was a serious slight to the Lord himself, which could not but incur his righteous anger.

Why did God chastise the Christians in Corinth? Because what they were doing was insulting to Christ and set aside God's known will (cf. James 2:10). The Supper encompasses a holy mystery that speaks of Christ and ministers grace to his people. Not to come reverently, discerning his body, is to *mock* the Saviour. Why should God not be offended and rise up in judgement?

Why did God judge the Corinthians?

We are so well schooled in the notion that God's love means his unconditional indulgence of every human sin, short of mass murder, that even a whisper of divine chastisement or judgement is greeted by frowns of disbelieving incomprehension. What used to be classed as 'sins' are now just called 'mistakes'. Everybody makes mistakes, after all. So how could anyone think God so mean-spirited and vindictive as to come down on people for commonplace infringements of the rules? The Corinthians, of course, were already experiencing God's judgement, so Paul was not speaking hypothetically, but after the fact. He was explaining why what had already happened had taken place. He therefore speaks successively about the *reality* of judgement, the *remedy* of judgement and the *reason* for judgement.

The reality of judgement (11:30)

'For this reason many are weak and sick among you, and many sleep,' says Paul. Illness is, of course, a commonplace experience of human beings. In a fallen world, people contract everything from colds to cancer. Furthermore, there is no reason to believe that every illness must be a judgement upon some particular sin. In the ordinary course of life, bad things happen to the best and worst apparently quite indiscriminately (Eccles. 9:2). The psalmist Asaph actually complains that notoriously godless people prosper in life and apparently have 'no pangs in their death', are of 'firm' strength and are not 'plagued' — that is, with sickness — 'like other men.' Only when he goes 'into the sanctuary of God' does he understand 'their end' (Ps. 73:4-5,17). He is reminded, by the existence of the temple sanctuary, that sacrifice has to be made for sinners, because sinners are lost and need to be saved by the grace of God. He gets his theology straight and gives up the simplistic theory that somehow only the bad should be ill, because bad things are not supposed to happen to good people.

This should not, however, lead us to dismiss the possibility that there sometimes are specific divine judgements annexed to particular, usually flagrant, sins. Our general response to afflictions ought certainly to be to reflect on our need of the Saviour (cf. Luke 13:1-5), but there may be occasions when there is compelling evidence for us to conclude that *this* affliction was a specific judgement for *that* sin. The only way we can know this is the case is if it may properly be deduced from the teaching of Scripture. For instance, the indulgence in wicked and self-destructive behaviour may well provide *prima facie* evidence of subsequent affliction being a judgement on that chosen manner of life. The Lord sometimes rather obviously humbles human pride in ways that seem too appropriate to the transgression to be merely coincidental.

Although very rare, there are a number of such instances recorded in Scripture. All of them remind us that God is not mocked and point us to some signal moral lesson. Not least, they serve advance notice that a greater accountability is yet to be faced before the bar of God's final judgement. Miriam was stricken with a (whitening) skin disease because she spoke against the (black) 'Ethiopian woman' whom Moses had married (Num. 12:10). Herod Agrippa I, having apparently entertained thoughts of his possible divinity, was 'eaten by worms and died' (Acts 12:23). The whole Israelite nation was judged by God for her idolatry in the desert wanderings: 'for wrath has gone out from the LORD. The plague has begun.' Only when Aaron stood between the living and the dead and offered atonement for the people was 'the plague ... stopped' (Num. 16:46-50).

In the present instance, Paul is infallibly interpreting the current experience of the Corinthian church. They were seeing people sicken and even die. This was more than the regular run of things. It was above the ordinary. It was pregnant with the displeasure of God.

John Calvin, observing the abuse of the Lord's Supper in his own day, observes: 'What a shocking mix-up there is, when no distinction is made [in admitting people to the Table, GJK], and scoundrels and people who were openly dissolute push their way in... And still we wonder what is the reason for so many wars, so many plagues, so many failures of the harvest, so many disasters and calamities, as if the cause were not in fact as plain as a pikestaff. And we certainly cannot look for an end to misfortunes, until we have removed their cause by correcting our faults.'[1]

God's judgements are, as the psalmist says, 'in all the earth' (Ps. 105:7). And the Corinthians had discovered that judgement must 'begin at the house of God' (1 Peter 4:17). Those who will not listen to God's Word will suffer the reminders of his wrath.

The remedy for judgement (11:31)

The remedy could have been applied in advance by simply 'discerning the Lord's body': 'For if we would judge ourselves, we would not be judged.' This is akin to the standard parental admonition to a child who has fallen into some trouble: 'If you had thought about what you were doing, you would not have got into this mess.' It is a fatherly word enjoining taking care ahead of time. The Corinthians would have saved themselves a lot of trouble, had they discerned the sinfulness of their attitudes and corrected their behaviour before they abused the Lord's Supper.

The reason for judgement (11:32)

The judgement had already been visited upon them, however, so any reformation needed to be after the fact rather than before it. It is at this point that Paul reveals the reason for these judgements: 'But when we are judged, we are chastened by the Lord, that we may not be condemned with the world.' R. C. H. Lenski observes that 'The Lord's judgements which he visits upon believers for the serious sins they commit are evidences of his fatherly love and not of damning wrath,' whereas, 'in the case of unbelievers the judgements which he visited upon them in this life are advance indications of his final consuming wrath.'[2] The same author notes that 'While chastisement is painful it still proves that we are children.' We have a Father who loves us enough to bring us back from self-destruction. God is the Father of his people. He loves them with an eternal purpose of grace. He will not let them go (cf. Heb. 12:5-11).

How to approach the Lord's Table

Were we invited to dinner at the White House or Buckingham Palace, we would take the greatest care to be respectful of our exalted hosts. We understand the importance of meeting with presidents and queens. But in the Lord's Supper we are invited to dine with the King of kings and Lord of lords! How much more, then, should we prepare our hearts and mind our manners, when we are called to sup with the Son of God! The Lord's Supper is no ordinary meal. The Lord Jesus Christ is no mere earthly ruler. He is the Saviour of the world. And he gave his life as the price of redeeming lost sinners like us. This commands attention to the matter of how we are properly to approach him at his Table.

The right attitude (11:33)

'Therefore, my brethren,' says Paul, 'when you come together to eat, wait for one another.' Here the apostle is referring to the original abuse of the Supper at Corinth, in which they had a communal meal, the 'love feast' or 'agape', prior to the communion. This feast was one in which all, from the rich to the slaves, shared in a meal which would have been provided mainly by those well-off enough to supply the food in sufficient quantity for the whole fellowship. This was designed to express unity. The way they did it, however, accomplished exactly the opposite (11:17-22). This spilled over into the Lord's Supper and sealed not only their disunity, but also their irreverence for Christ and the Lord's Supper. Whenever they came together as a church 'to eat' (regular meals), they were to 'wait for one another', that is, they were not to start eating before others and turn the thing into little better than a bacchanalia!

Faithful participation in the Lord's Supper requires due preparation of the heart. Not least, it demands that the whole community of faith come together in the exercise of love for Christ and for each other. It is striking that Paul does not say, 'when you come together to *sit at the Lord's Table*'. The problem was not simply that they abused the Lord's Supper and needed to brush up on their etiquette for that particular observance. Attitude comes before etiquette. Their problem was comprehensive and spiritual. They needed repentance and renewal from the heart, with application to every aspect of their life as a congregation of professing Christian people.

The right action (11:34)

'If anyone is hungry, let him eat at home, lest you come together for judgement.' The point here is that no one should come to either the love feasts or the Lord's Supper just because he is hungry. Neither meal was designed merely to fill the stomach. Even the church meal, the 'love feast', was not meant to be a charity dinner — a kind of ecclesiastical soup kitchen to feed the poor among the faithful. The twin goals of these meals were unity and fellowship. The Lord's Supper, of course, was a symbolic meal with a sacramental purpose directed to the spiritual blessing and growth of the communicants. So neither the love feast nor the Lord's Supper was to be regarded as an ordinary meal.

The right guidance (11:34)

Paul's final statement can easily be passed over as an ephemeral, if apostolic, footnote. When he says, 'And the rest I will set in order when I come,' he not only states what he will do when he gets to Corinth, but points to the abiding fact that God has provided leadership and guidance for his church. There are no more apostles today, but the Lord has still given government to the church. The elders are to set things in order according to the Word of God. Each believer is to come to the Table in such a way that he or she discerns the Lord's body. Each individual is responsible for his own attitude and actions in receiving the sacrament.

The church, however, has a corporate responsibility, through her elders, to set things in order. The elders cannot read the hearts of their people, but they can assess the credibility of their confessions of faith and the consistency of their daily lives. It is a mark of a true church, as a body acting through her elders, that the sacraments be faithfully administered. That cannot be confined merely to the observance of the correct outward form of the sacrament — the proper officers reading the appropriate Scripture and passing out the correct sacramental elements. God's people must also be exhorted from God's Word so that their consciences are challenged as to the imperatives of holy obedience to the will of the Lord. This should also aim to encourage their hearts as to the promise of joyous communion with Christ in a Supper that portrays the very heart of his saving work on their behalf.

On the other hand, the ungodly must be prevented from coming to the Table and the godly only admitted when they have shown by profession of faith before the church and a consistent life before both church and world that they truly do 'discern the Lord's body'.

7.
Communion

'The cup of blessing which we bless, is it not the communion of the body of Christ...?' (1 Cor.10:16).

The feasts and festivals of the Old Testament period were meticulously detailed and given impressive titles ('Day of Atonement', 'Feast of Tabernacles,' etc.). Yet the one and only prescribed feast of the New Testament church is given no official title in God's Word and is described, first by our Lord and then by the apostle Paul, in terms of the simplest instructions, devoid of all pomp and show.

The nearest we come to a title is the expression in our text, 'the communion', and this is what has stuck, at least across the Protestant world. Even then, it is clear that this is no formal title, but more a practical exposition of what the Lord's Supper (as we call it) is meant to be for the followers of Jesus. Of course, we have to give everything a name. The term 'Lord's Supper' refers simultaneously to the fact that the Lord instituted it and to the occasion of its institution, the Last Supper before the crucifixion of Christ. 'Communion,' as we have noted, is drawn from

Paul's definition of the import of the Supper for the experience of the church as a body. Others, especially Roman Catholicism and 'high church' Episcopalianism, have tended to prefer the term 'the Eucharist', from the Greek *eucharisteo* (to give thanks), which refers to the Lord's praying to set apart the bread as a symbol of his broken body.

'Communion' emphasizes *koinonia* in Christ, the priesthood of all believers, each in direct fellowship with Christ. 'Eucharist,' on the other hand, focuses on blessing from Christ and thankfulness for the ministration of grace through the provision of Christ as Saviour. These words are both biblical, as are the concepts encapsulated in their precise meaning.

It is perhaps worth observing that these terms — communion and Eucharist — seem somehow to tie in with what those who favour them appear to think is most central to the Supper. It is interesting that ritualistic, hierarchical churches that multiply sacraments administered by the clergy as a mediating priesthood favour the term 'Eucharist'. The sacerdotal system of Rome interposes ecclesiastical mediators who dispense the blessing of automatic *(ex opere operato)* grace in the distribution of the 'host' (the bread made into flesh). Those who favour 'communion' tend to be those who also reject a mediating priesthood for a non-hierarchical ministry and a priesthood of all believers. The Reformed faith understands that there is one mediator between God and man, Jesus, and that through faith in him, the believer communes with him, *sans* mass, *sans* priests, *sans* any other mediator.

What our text lays out for us is the fundamental definition of what the Lord's Supper is to be for those who are properly to come to it. It is a *communion* in Jesus, on account of his death as an atoning sacrifice for the sin of sinners he is saving. The vital concern is *koinonia* (communion, fellowship, participation) with God, in and through Jesus his Son.

Communion with Jesus Christ

The Lord's Supper has, in too many churches and perhaps also in the perception of the watching world, become a piece of religious pageantry, with mysterious but otherwise unfelt and dimly understood significance for those who participate. In some circles, it has been reduced to the minimal involvement that maintains the other privileges of church membership. Attend a communion once a year and you will be guaranteed Christian burial and some hope of salvation. Any reading of the biblical teaching on the Supper and the nature of saving faith in Jesus Christ surely exposes such notions as a caricature of the real thing, if not, indeed, a blasphemous parody of the gospel itself. The focus of the Lord's Supper is squarely upon personal and experiential communion with the crucified and risen Jesus.

An experienced communion

The text establishes this essential perspective through its two main points.

1. The 'cup of blessing which we bless' is the wine as set apart in prayer for sacramental use. Just as we ought to pray before meals that God would bless the food to our body's use, so we ask a blessing to the end that the elements of bread and wine fulfil their intended purpose in our lives. The dynamic of divine presence and power is invoked. Why? So that our use of the symbols of Christ's body and blood would not be allowed to degenerate into perfunctory ritual or mere pageantry, however subjectively and emotionally meaningful. Furthermore, so that we would understand that going to the Lord's Table is to mean more than some general feeling of having done something Jesus wanted us to do, although we privately thought it a strange thing to be doing.

The point is that God means to meet with his people in the sacrament, that there is content to the communion and that it is consciously received in terms of a saving knowledge of Christ.

2. This, in turn, leads in to the consideration that the purpose of participation in the Supper is 'a communion of the blood of Christ'. As with the Word of God itself, the body and blood of Christ must be received by faith. There must be a believing heart for there to be an experience of true communion. Why? Because the Supper is not a delivery system for automatic grace to all who may come and participate. It is not the physical reception of Christ's flesh and blood that is in view, but a spiritual feeding of the soul upon him. And that which is truly spiritual is explicitly experiential. We feed on Christ in the sacrament in the same basic way that we feed on him in the Word of God, namely

through the exercise of a living faith, from our hearts, in him as the risen Saviour.

A communion experience

Given that the Lord's Supper is designed to be an experience of union and communion with Christ, what impact does this have on our Christian experience in practice, as we come to the Table? Bearing in mind what we have already seen in these studies, several points suggest themselves as essential to the communion experience.

1. Do you come to the Table properly *discerning the Lord's body*? (1 Cor. 11:29). This was the subject of the previous study and we need not repeat all that has already been said on the subject. Suffice it to say that it is essential to a living communion with Jesus Christ that the communicant comes with a consciousness of his own appropriation of Christ, as the one who died to save him from his sins. 'We receive and appropriate Him as our sacrifice and as the Saviour of our souls; and He gives Himself to us. It is therefore an act of intimate communion.'[1]

2. Do you come to the Table in the conviction that it is *a seal of the covenant of grace* — and therefore a channel of grace communicating to you the benefits of Christ's death? Those who come to God 'must believe that he is, and that he is a rewarder of those who diligently seek him' (Heb. 11:6). Believing is the necessary condition of receiving. Yet there are some who, for example, 'try prayer'

and wait to see 'if it works'. That is more in line with the mercenary spirit of Simon Magus than the true spirit of prayer that trusts in the Lord and his promises. To approach the Lord's Table in a similar way, as if 'to see what it does for me', when in my heart there is neither heartfelt devotion nor confiding expectation is consumerism, not covenant-faithfulness. You must *believe* if you are to be *blessed*.

3. Do you come to the Table realizing that the sacrament *glories in the cross of Christ*, and that you must also do so as you come? In this, writes Henry Belfrage, '... we show that, instead of participating in the contempt with which others regard the death of Christ, we glory in His cross. The crucifixion of Christ ... was ... the object of ridicule and opposition... To trust for salvation in one who had been crucified through weakness ... and to proclaim a suffering criminal as the most illustrious of characters — seemed to the carnal and perverted mind, the height of madness. In opposition to such ideas ... Christians were, by the observance of this ordinance, to show that they saw everything in the cross which could call forth triumphant exaltation... In Thy cross, O Jesus, is my salvation and my glory; the rock of my strength and my refuge is in Thee.'[2]

4. Do you come to the Table, having *prepared your heart* to receive the blessings Christ will give? Those who come expecting nothing will not be disappointed. No preparation is preparation for nothing. And nothing will be the

result. Worse, unprepared hearts are careless hearts and careless hearts are hardening hearts! If you come eagerly, humbly, with a believing and loving heart, then the Lord will confirm his promises to your soul and give you a wider, deeper and higher view of his glory.

5. In summary, we are to come to the Table *in order to have fellowship with Jesus Christ himself.* The Supper presents Christ's death in terms of the symbols of bread and wine. Jesus is truly present in the Supper. He communicates his grace to his people in the Supper. Living communion with Christ and actual reception of spiritual blessings are experienced by all who, having a true saving faith in Christ, participate in a worthy manner in this sacrament of his death for sinners.

Communion with fellow-believers

No Christian is called to be a kind of religious 'lone ranger'. True communion with Christ carries with it a desire — not merely an obligation — to commune with the 'body of Christ'. There is a transition from the bread as a symbol of Christ's physical body (1 Cor. 10:16) to the church as a whole as the body of Christ (10:17). Christ's body is broken so that those he saves may be melded into one body in him. In terms of the symbolism of the Supper, the bread, which is the Redeemer, is broken to make the redeemed into a single loaf.

Communion with one another

The Lord's Supper, then, is not an exercise in individualism. You will often hear people say that their faith is a matter between them and their God. This is how many excuse their unwillingness to discuss what they believe. It is how some justify their not joining a church, so avoiding accountability to the ministry of pastor and elders. It is how others, in the case of the Lord's Supper, can regard it to be their unquestioned right to participate without any accountability to their supposed brothers and sisters in Christ for the consistency or otherwise of their lives as professing Christians. Let it be said, clearly and unequivocally, that the Bible nowhere allows the view that your faith is only and exclusively a matter between God and you. This is a self-serving modern myth. It denies the essential corporate element in the approval, the conduct and the growth of Christian faith and life. In Scripture, those who go it alone invariably go wrong. People can go it alone in groups, of course. The issue is the role of the church, not the number of people involved. Ananias and Sapphira did things their way; Simon Magus also. The Corinthian factions ('I am ...of Apollos ... of Paul,' etc.) refused submission to the corporate imperatives of Christian faith and life. Hence the apostle's emphasis on the church as a body with different interdependent parts (1 Cor. 12).

The corporate dimension in the Lord's Supper is exemplified in the fact, clearly set forth in our text, that there are *three* parties involved: God in Christ, the believer and other believers. It is not a case of 'him and me,' but of 'him, me and you (plural)'! This, not coincidentally, is why the Lord's Supper is given to the church to administer, and not to the individual Christian to self-administer. You cannot administer the Supper to yourself, neither can you admit yourself to the Table, because it is given to the church as a whole, for the deepening of spiritual growth and fellowship with Christ in the body as a whole. This is why the Lord has given its administration to the church, according to his institution, with God-appointed elders who either admit or refuse individuals who would come to the Table on the basis of the credibility of their profession of faith and the consistency of their walk with the Lord. 'For we, though many, are one bread and one body; for we all partake of that one bread.' The Supper is an ordinance of the visible church, not of individuals who autonomously decide that they will participate. It is corporate in nature and is an act of communion with fellow-believers in the context of the church as instituted by Christ and its government by elders.

Practising communion with one another

This implies that we recognize and practise the common bond that binds all who believe in the Lord Jesus Christ and are saved by his grace. The Christian is not one island in an archipelago called the church. He is a part of a contiguous territory — the visible church — whose builder and maker is God.

Although there is an invisible aspect to the church, in that it comprises people both on earth and in heaven, and encompasses people scattered among different churches, the fact remains that there is no such thing as a meeting of the invisible church. And there is no such thing as a sacrament of the invisible church.

The church exists, whatever its size, wherever Christ has called together a people and they are organized with a plurality of elders he has raised up. A family is not a church. A hermit is not a church. A collection of individuals is not a church. A church is a body, where there are members who acknowledge themselves for what they are, and submit to Christ and to one another in terms of the gifts and graces and ministries he has given to them. Individuals who attend a church but hold aloof from commitment to that body and submission to the elders over that body in holy things are simulating church membership, even playing church, and in effect reserving to themselves the authority that is Christ's and that Christ has given to his body. The Lord's Supper is where, among other things, Christians practise their recognition of their brothers and sisters in Christ, and commit themselves to go on to grow in mutual submission as members one of another (1 Cor. 12:27).

This calls us to review in our hearts our relationships with our brothers and sisters in the church — and not the church in some ethereal, theoretical, cosmic sense, but the church where we worship. Face the implications directly and personally. Do you love the people in the congregation where you worship? Do you know an appreciable number of them? Is that church somewhere you go to satisfy a naked sense of obligation to worship God, or is it a body of which you desire and love to be a part, and where you truly worship God in Spirit and in truth? (John 4:24). Are there unresolved, unrepented sins and obstacles between you and others in that fellowship? Are you seeking reconciliation (as per Matthew 18:15-20), or do you just avoid these folk and keep to your comfortable clique of like-minded friends? Are you committed to building enduring bonds of friendship and fellowship with fellow-Christians?

Can you expect Christ to commune with you, if your answers to these questions are determinedly at variance with his known will? Anyone who is content to keep aloof from the life of the body, either by despising other Christians or denying the authority and ministerial leading of the church through her ministers and elders, has no promise from the Lord of blessing at the Table or, for that matter, anywhere else. That is a hard saying, but it is an inescapable truth. All who desire to come to the Lord's Table and enjoy the blessing of the Lord are also already living in communion with the Lord and in fellowship with his people. Where there are problems, they are committed to resolving them through the means the Lord has given to the church.

Because Christians glory in the cross (Gal. 6:14), they love to come to Christ together. They draw great encouragement from the unity that grows in and even through their very diversity. They delight in the way Jesus has blessed other believers. They praise God for the communion of the saints and look forward to glory, when heaven will be filled with brothers and sisters in Jesus Christ. Then, together made perfect in holiness, they will all enjoy the unclouded communion of the eternal marriage supper of the Lamb, who was slain to take away the sin of the world.

Notes

Chapter 1 — Consecration

1. Charles Hodge, *Princeton Sermons,* p.373.
2. Thomas Doolittle, *A Treatise concerning the Lord's Supper,* p.8.
3. Hodge, *Princeton Sermons,* p.332.
4. See C. Hodge, *Systematic Theology,* vol. III, pp.647-50.
5. Henry Belfrage, *Sacramental Addresses and Meditations,* p.337.

Chapter 2 — Visible signs

1. See *Shorter Catechism,* question 88.
2. Doolittle, *The Lord's Supper,* pp.32-3.
3. *Rutherford's Catechism: containing the Sum of the Christian Religion,* p.79.
4. As above, pp.79-80.
5. Cf. *Westminster Larger Catechism,* 169.
6. Herman Hoeksema, *The Triple Knowledge: an exposition of the Heidelberg Catechism,* vol. 2, p.459.

Chapter 3 — The presence of Christ

1. Philip Henry, *Christ All in All,* Reiner Publications, Swengel, PA, 1970.
2. Charles Hodge, *I Corinthians,* p.226.

Chapter 4 — Proclaiming the Lord's death

1. Belfrage, *Sacramental Addresses,* p.336.
2. Hodge, *I Corinthians,* vol. 1, p.229.
3. Thomas Manton, *Complete Works,* vol. XVIII: pp.328-9.

Chapter 5 — Self-examination

1. Charles Simeon, *Expository Outlines,* vol. 16, p.295.
2. Doolittle, *The Lord's Supper,* p.50.
3. Simeon, *Expository Outlines,* vol. 16, pp.294-5.

Chapter 6 — Discerning the Lord's body
1. John Calvin, *I Corinthians,* p.255.
2. R. C. H. Lenski, *First Corinthians,* p.485.

Chapter 7 — Communion
1. Hodge, *Princeton Sermons,* p.330.
2. Belfrage, *Sacramental Addresses,* p.337.